engaging in the rendering of legal, financial, medical or professional advice. The content within this book has been derived from various sources. Please consult a licensed professional before attempting any techniques outlined in this book.

By reading this document, the reader agrees that under no circumstances is the author responsible for any losses, direct or indirect, which are incurred as a result of the use of information contained within this document, including, but not limited to, — errors, omissions, or inaccuracies.

Table of Contents

3

Algorithmic Trading

Complete beginner's guide to learning algorithmic trading strategies
Written by SOPHIA FOSTER

"Algorithmic Trading Systems: Advanced Gap
Strategies for the Futures
Markets" is a practical automated trading systems
book."

Mark J. Pa
*Professional
Investor*

Table of Contents

CFTC DISCLOSURES & DISCLAIMERS

HYPOTHETICAL PERFORMANCE RESULTS HAVE MANY INHERENT LIMITATIONS, SOME OF WHICH ARE DESCRIBED BELOW. NO REPRESENTATION IS BEING MADE THAT ANY ACCOUNT WILL OR IS LIKELY TO ACHIEVE PROFITS OR LOSSES SIMILAR TO THOSE SHOWN; IN FACT, THERE ARE FREQUENTLY SHARP DIFFERENCES BETWEEN HYPOTHETICAL PERFORMANCE RESULTS AND THE ACTUAL RESULTS SUBSEQUENTLY ACHIEVED BY ANY PARTICULAR TRADING PROGRAM. ONE OF THE LIMITATIONS OF HYPOTHETICAL PERFORMANCE RESULTS IS THAT THEY ARE GENERALLY PREPARED WITH THE BENEFIT OF HINDSIGHT. IN ADDITION, HYPOTHETICAL TRADING DOES NOT INVOLVE FINANCIAL RISK, AND NO HYPOTHETICAL TRADING RECORD CAN COMPLETELY ACCOUNT FOR THE IMPACT OF FINANCIAL RISK OF ACTUAL TRADING. FOR EXAMPLE, THE ABILITY TO WITHSTAND LOSSES OR TO ADHERE TO A PARTICULAR TRADING PROGRAM IN SPITE OF TRADING LOSSES ARE MATERIAL POINTS WHICH CAN ALSO ADVERSELY AFFECT ACTUAL TRADING RESULTS. THERE ARE NUMEROUS OTHER FACTORS RELATED TO THE

MARKETS IN GENERAL OR TO THE IMPLEMENTATION OF ANY SPECIFIC TRADING PROGRAM WHICH CANNOT BE FULLY ACCOUNTED FOR IN THE PREPARATION OF HYPOTHETICAL PERFORMANCE RESULTS AND ALL WHICH CAN ADVERSELY AFFECT TRADING RESULTS.

THESE PERFORMANCE TABLES AND RESULTS ARE HYPOTHETICAL IN NATURE AND DO NOT REPRESENT TRADING IN ACTUAL ACCOUNTS.

1.   Introduction

"Algorithmic Trading Systems: Advanced Gap Strategies for the Futures Markets" is a practical automated trading systems book. We reveal the open code in the book and the exact algorithms we use in the book are available for download from the companion website. The code for both Tradestation and NinjaTrader can be downloaded. Instructional videos are also included on the companion website. This is one of the more "hands on" trading systems books you will read since it includes the code for multiple platforms. The Tradestation EasyLanguage code can also be use in MultiCharts while NinjaTrader uses C# and .Net in the NinjaScript editor. I highly recommend using one of these platforms while reading this book. Chapter 16 includes the details on how to access the website and videos as well as the links for the trading platforms.

This book uses a straight forward and direct approach for communicating the details of algorithmic trading systems. We don't use fancy theoretical formulas to talk about the market but take a practical approach to what I have found works best in the markets after 20 years of research and trading. When studying top traders and market wizards, most cite a simple approach to the market and discovering market inefficiencies based on market observations.

We start in Chapter 2 by building on our book "Seven Trading Systems for the S&P Futures" published in 2010. In "Seven Trading Systems for the S&P Futures", basic gap strategies were developed as we discussed trading systems specifically for the E-mini S&P futures using the Tradestation Platform. In "Algorithmic Trading Systems" we expand the discussion to additional trading platforms and additional markets including the German Bund and 24 hour markets such as the Euro Currency. We discuss how to find gap patterns and strategies for 24 hour markets by using Custom Sessions.

In Chapter 4, we introduce a new pattern that provides us with a trading opportunity after the gap has been filled. Sometimes a Gap Fill can happen quickly and is done within the first few minutes of trading. If trading gap fills is the only strategy you are using, your trading could be done for the day. This new pattern provides additional opportunities in the market after the gap fill. We reveal the best way to trade this strategy using either stop or limit entry orders in the E-mini S&P, DAX, Euro Currency, and Crude Oil.

In the middle of the book, starting in Chapter 8, we offer a detailed explanation of Trading System Principles that are very important in our strategy development. We talk about how to interpret famous Wall Street trading axioms such as, "You can't go broke taking profits" (indeed you can!) and "Do not let a winning trade turn into a loser". We challenge these "pearls of wisdom" and explain common misconceptions about trading systems principles that are tricky to apply and understand when developing trading systems. We take a look at how to test limit orders and how to set stop losses and profit targets.

Towards the end of the book, starting in Chapter 14, we add advanced techniques to our new pattern by discussing multiple exit strategies and multiple trend filtering rules as well as some coding techniques in Chapter 15.

Gap strategies offer one of the best examples of how trading psychology works in the market and provides us with a great basis for the stability behind our trading systems. Gaps can quickly reverse at the open and fill the gap by moving to the previous day's close and then, once the gap has been filled (or almost filled), the market can then reverse again and go in the original direction of the gap. There are different groups of traders ranging from floor/exchange based traders, to large speculators, to the retail trader all who react at different price points with the goal of capturing short term trends during the day based on different support and resistance points that include the opening and closing values for which gap patterns are based on.

This book is written for traders who are interested in automated trading systems using a specific set of rules or algorithm. The content is technical and includes specific rules from trading systems as well as advanced programming code. We believe as traders it is important to have a very well defined approach to trading beyond just a general indicator based method. There are many methods that are shared and sold in the trading world and in trader education courses, but without an exact set of rules that can be converted into an automated trading system, it can be very difficult to achieve the same results as another trading "pro" who shares an indicator method that requires individual interpretation. It is not possible to actually determine if those indicator based methods actually work or if you fully understand them the way they are being taught without converting those "specific rules" to a trading system. I see many good ideas and methods that I have programmed into an automated trading system and back tested and the results do not hold up. The author of those methods may be a successful and profitable trader with good intentions but uses additional subconscious inputs from the market to determine exactly when to employ each method. Unless you can take all the same trades, it can be difficult to get the same results.

The benefit of this book is that it does provide specific methods with measureable results that can be monitored historically as well as the ability to look at future walk forward results in order to see how the trading systems would have performed since they were released. It would be easier to show a general indicator method and some cherry picked trades and show a few examples of how well each cherry picked trade or trading period worked. An accurately tested trading system does not lie about historical results. While there is no guarantee that the system will be profitable in the future, based on changing market conditions and price action, I prefer a specific set of measurable rules to manage a portfolio of trading systems with the knowledge that some of the trading systems may incur a worse case draw down. The alternative is to "fly by the seat of the pants" with a method where we are unsure of how our setup would work in all market conditions.

It is easy to see a pattern that works for a week and then try to trade that pattern for the next month, only to realize it was a mirage and that the more we observe the pattern, the more rules we add or additional patterns that we begin to notice. This prevents us from being consistent and can cause a trader to jump from one idea to the next quickly burning through a trading account. We don't have a road map of expectations without a specific strategy that allows us to measure results. If you go into a drawdown using a discretionary method, how do you know when to stop? With a trading system we can see historically where we are in the drawdown curve and determine if a system is no longer working based on the drawdown or consecutive losers.

I do believe it is possible to be a screen trader or tape reader and to be profitable. This is a skill that I work to develop. I do believe this skill is difficult to develop and very rare. I believe that starting with automated trading systems is one way to potentially "graduate" to becoming a discretionary trader since discretionary trading would require the same discipline and consistency that an automated trading system could provide. You never get to the point where you can just show up on the trading scene and trade by the "seat of the pants" and achieve long term consistent results.

For traders with extra capital and time, working on developing discretionary trading skills by testing manual techniques will also provide additional insight into the market. It has helped me develop my trading systems by intimately knowing the market in real time instead of just data mining static or historical data. This approach can help a trader "see" the market better which will help develop a general method followed by the progression of developing a trading system. This can be a capital intensive approach and the amount of money I have spent testing trading systems in real time using manual approaches is well over $100,000 (in the form of trading losses in order to test ideas in real time). The cost of developing profitable strategies can be high since most ideas don't work. Developing strategies on static data or market replay is still a very good method to use, requiring much less capital. The later is the approach we focus on in this book.

We use the term Algorithmic to mean a rules based approach. The definition in Dictionary.com is, "A finite set of unambiguous instructions performed in a prescribed sequence to achieve a goal, especially a mathematical rule or procedure used to compute a desired result. Algorithms are the basis for most computer programming. A set of instructions for solving a problem, especially on a computer."

This book is not about high frequency trading. We use simple ideas. We do not discuss advanced mathematics or statistics. A large percentage of the trading systems that I have developed over the years are low frequency trading systems and pattern based. Trying to use a delayed mathematical representation of the market in the form of an indicator as the primary entry technique is a linear approach that I have not found to be profitable in most cases (there are always exceptions). I have found that repeating price patterns tend to capture trading psychology much better. I have also found that when using lower frequency patterns I am not competing with the market makers and high frequency traders. The market has the tendency to "destroy" inefficiencies. I believe that this is how many of the higher frequency quantitative strategies are intentionally developed. They find inefficiencies in the market and fade the trades that are working so well, correcting them back to a state of mean reversion and market efficiency. If you find an inefficiency that occurs 1-4 times per month, the market will not catch it and destroy it as quickly as a high frequency inefficiency that occurs daily or several times per day.

Another benefit of this book is that it provides a resource for experienced traders to study another trader's research. It is important to always be learning and expanding what we know and to see what other market participants can see and will consider in their trading decisions so that we can either be contrarian or follow the trend of that inefficiency. I enjoy reading trading system books written by other traders in order to expand my thinking. As a trader becomes more experienced, taking the work of one trader and incorporating it into what you know about the markets, and making changes based on your own observations can be very powerful.

This book can benefit a trader at any level, from beginner to advanced, as well as those who are discretionary traders since we know discretionary traders base their decisions on facts they have found to be true about the market. This book covers many facts that we have found to be true about the market.

This book is not a book that covers every aspect of trading. I personally don't believe I could ever finish a book that tried to cover every aspect of trading as my insights grow more quickly than I can write and publish them. It is a small snap shot of what I know but a very good snap shot that includes detailed information with open code trading systems that can be imported directly into your trading platform and traded live if the strategies meet your risk criteria.

This book is not for the casual reader seeking general financial advice, economic theory, or dramatic trading stories. It is for the hands on technical trader interested in developing skills related to trading systems. The EasyLanguage and C# code are included on the companion website. There are many career opportunities for those seeking careers with trading firms that require C# programming skills. It generally takes an experienced programmer to work for a trading firm but this can be a start or step in that direction for those aspiring to learn code in order to work for a trading firm.

Price discovery, market research, and trading are my professional passions. I enjoy the process of solving the constantly moving and changing puzzle we call the "market". Coming from a family of educators, writing and publishing are also one of my passions and interests. Writing this book has taken a few years as I have worked on it off and on. Many of the statements, screen shots, images, and examples can take place between the years from 2012 – 2015. I hope that you enjoy reading "Algorithmic Trading Systems" and find it to be a useful resource to add to your trading.

2.   Gap Fills in the Euro Currency

One of my favorite markets to trade is the Euro Currency. The Euro Currency futures trade "virtually" 24 hours per day from Sunday at 6 pm EST until Friday at 5 pm EST. I say "virtually" because the Euro Currency futures which are traded on the CME, closes for an hour each day from 5pm-6pm EST while the cash/forex remains open during this timeframe. Even, though the Euro Currency trades around the clock, it is most active between 2 am-12 noon EST, during Europe's business day.

To capture this window of volume, we create a custom session to isolate the price action during this timeframe. This custom timeframe will eliminate the lower volume and lower range bars in the less active timeframe for this market so that our calculations will only compare the price and volume during the more active timeframe for this market that includes the higher volume and higher range bars. In the image below, we show how volume picks up at 2 am EST. This is also the time when the DAX, Euro Stoxx, Euro Bund futures in Germany open for trading on the EUREX.

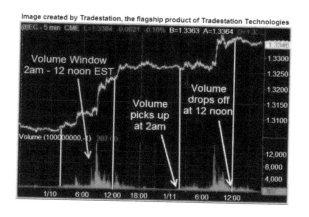

Figure 2-1

In this chapter, we show how to create a custom session and setup our Euro Gap Fill trading system in the Tradestation and NinjaTrader Platform.

Theory

This strategy setup is very powerful. Whenever there is a gap in the opposite direction of the trend, the market can have a tendency to move in the direction of the original trend. In the Euro Currency, the European business day opens at 2 am EST or New York Time. If the trend has been up and all of a sudden Europe opens the business day and market participants observe lower prices in the Euro, the instant reaction could be to buy

19

value. This would be an opportunity for commercials who are buying "product" from European distributors the opportunity to get a "discount" from the previous day's prices. The opposite scenario is true if the Euro Currency is weak, market participants have a chance to sell Euros at much higher prices on a gap up. The concept is based on short term trend deviations and mean reversion.

There are many different ways to determine the direction of the trend. In this strategy, we use the MACD indicator. MACD means Moving Average Convergence Divergence. This indicator can be used to determine the trend by tracking the difference between two different exponential moving average lengths as well as the average of the difference.

In the image below we can see a daily chart of the Euro Currency futures continuous contract (@EC) in the Tradestation platform. The histogram changes between green and red. It represents the MACD and the exponential moving average of MACD. When it is green the MACD is greater than the exponential moving average of MACD. When it is red, the MACD is less than the exponential moving average of MACD. When the histogram is green, the trend is up and we take long trades. When the histogram is red, the trend is down and we take short trades. We use the daily chart as data 2 to measure MACD while data1 is a five minute chart in this strategy. We reference data2 for the MACD measurement but place trades on data1 so that we can trade a smaller time interval for more precise entries.

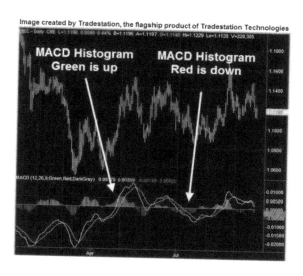

Figure 2-2

The Strategy

In this section we will define the specific rules of the strategy by listing the rules for the trade setups.

<u>For Long Entries:</u>

    1.)   If it is the first bar of the new session and the Open of the first bar of this session is less than the Close of the previous session and the trend is up, then we enter at the next five minute bar.

2.)   This strategy uses a Custom Session from 2 am - 1 pm EST so that the close of the previous session is 1 pm EST and the open of the current session is 2 am EST. This strategy uses five minute bars.

3.)   The trend is defined by the MACD Histogram being greater than zero.

4.)   The strategy enters at 2:05 am EST if there is a trade. If there is no trade at 2:05 am EST then the strategy does not take a trade for the day. The maximum number of trades that can be taken each day is one. The Stop Loss is $500 while the profit target is $250 for trades where the Open is within the previous day's range of the custom session. There is no profit target used if the open is outside of the previous day's range. The strategy will also exit by 12 noon EST if it is still in a trade.

For Short Entries:

1.) If it is the first bar of the new session and the Open of the first bar of this session is greater than the Close of the previous session and the trend is down, then we enter at the next five minute bar at 2:05 am EST.

2.) This strategy uses a Custom Session from 2 am - 1 pm EST so that the close of the previous session is 1 pm EST and the open of the current session is 2 am EST. This strategy uses five minute bars.

3.) The trend is defined by the MACD Histogram being less than zero.

4.) The strategy enters at 2:05 am if there is a trade. If there is no trade then the strategy does not take a trade for the day. The maximum number of trades that can be taken each day is one. The Stop Loss is $500 while the profit target is $200 for trades where the Open is in within the previous day's range of the custom session. There is no profit target used if the open is outside of the previous day's range. The strategy will also exit by 12 noon EST if it is still in a trade.

The Code

Next we take the rules from our strategy and specifically program them into Tradestation EasyLanguage.

```
18 { ** Copyright (c) 1986-2016 Capstone Trading Systems All rights reserved. ** }

Inputs: cntrcts(1), MaxDailyEntries(1),
        FastLength( 12 ), SlowLength( 26 ), MACDLength( 9 ),
        StpLs(500), PrfTg(250),
        ExTime(1200);

Vars: MyMACD( 0 ), MACDAvg( 0 ), MACDDiff( 0 ) ;

MyMACD = MACD(Close of data2, FastLength, SlowLength ) ;
MACDAvg = XAverage( MyMACD, MACDLength ) ;
MACDDiff = MyMACD - MACDAvg ;

If Date<>Date[1]
   and EntriesToday(date)<MaxDailyEntries
   and Open>Close[1] = 0
   and MyMACD<MACDAvg
   Then Sell Short ("EuroGap SE") cntrcts contracts Next Bar at market;

If Date<>Date[1]
   and EntriesToday(date)<MaxDailyEntries
   and Open<Close[1] = 0
   and MyMACD>MACDAvg
   Then Buy ("EuroGap LE") cntrcts contracts Next Bar at market;

SetStopContract;
SetStopLoss(StpLs);

If OpenD(0)>CloseD(1) and OpenD(0)<HighD(1) Then SetProfitTarget(PrfTg);
If OpenD(0)<CloseD(1) and OpenD(0)>LowD(1) Then SetProfitTarget(PrfTg);

If Time=ExTime Then Sell Next Bar at market;
If Time=ExTime Then Buy to Cover Next Bar at Market;
SetExitOnClose;
```

Figure 2-3

Performance Reports

Whenever we design a trading system we take a look at the hypothetical performance summary to determine how the strategy has performed in the past. There is never a guarantee that future performance will match past performance. Understanding the past and developing strategies on historical data is a place to start. We look for strategies that work well without optimization and have a behavior that can be explained. This approach can be very valuable when it is also used with money management and with continued walk forward analysis from the initial design of the strategy to see how well the strategy performs in the future as compared to the past.

24

The next set of images show the performance summary from the Tradestation platform. The results do not include transaction costs such as slippage or commission. We will be using the continuous contracts when testing strategies. The data and input settings screen shots as well as an analysis of the results will be discussed after the performance summaries.

TradeStation Performance Summary   Expand »

All Trades

Total Net Profit	$48,487.50	Profit Factor	1.30
Gross Profit	$209,137.50	Gross Loss	($160,650.00)
Total Number of Trades	997	Percent Profitable	63.79%
Winning Trades	636	Losing Trades	357
Even Trades	4		
Avg. Trade Net Profit	$48.63	Ratio Avg. Win:Avg. Loss	0.73
Avg. Winning Trade	$328.83	Avg. Losing Trade	($450.00)
Largest Winning Trade	$5,037.50	Largest Losing Trade	($500.00)
Max. Consecutive Winning Trades	12	Max. Consecutive Losing Trades	6
Avg. Bars in Winning Trades	43.18	Avg. Bars in Losing Trades	54.47
Avg. Bars in Total Trades	47.53		
Max. Shares/Contracts Held	1	Account Size Required	$4,062.50
Return on Initial Capital	48.49%	Annual Rate of Return	4.45%
Return Retracement Ratio	0.15	RINA Index	1524.19
Trading Period	8 Yrs, 10 Mths, 18 Dys, 6 Hrs, 45 Mins	Percent of Time in the Market	4.98%
Max. Equity Run-up	$55,125.00		

Max. Drawdown (Intra-day Peak to Valley)		**Max. Drawdown (Trade Close to Trade Close)**	
Value	($4,662.50)	Value	($4,062.50)
Net Profit as % of Drawdown	1039.95%	Net Profit as % of Drawdown	1193.54%
Max. Trade Drawdown	($500.00)		

Equity Curve Line - @EC 5 min.(07/03/06 02:05 - 05/22/15 13:00)

Figure 2-4

The data settings for this strategy include a custom session. To setup the custom session in Tradestation go to Format, Symbol and select the Properties tab. The name of the custom session that we use is EURO MORNING. This session is from 1 am to 12 noon

26

CST and based on the exchange time. Even if your computer is on a different time zone than CST, the custom session is still based on the exchange time. The screen shots below from Tradestation show the settings for this. To setup this custom session, simply select Create in the second screen shot and set it up as shown in the image. We used the name EURO MORNING but any name could be used.

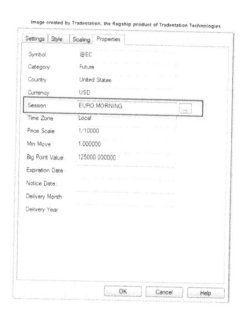

Figure 2-5

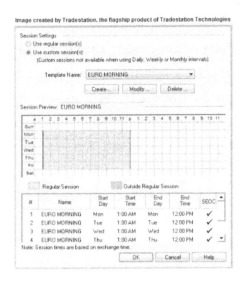

Figure 2-6

The performance summaries can give us a roadmap for future expectations for the type of performance we expect if the strategy continues to work going forward. The worse case drawdown and maximum consecutive losers are keys to knowing what to expect in a worst case scenario for risk management. It is common to have a worse case drawdown and for the strategy to bounce back. It can also be common for a strategy to continue into a worse case drawdown and discontinue working based on changes in the market. Understanding the market and the strategy, can help determine what percent of the worse case drawdown would allow us to stop trading the system. Many new traders can be impatient and quit after 3-5 consecutive losers even if the performance report shows us that the strategy has incurred 8-10 consecutive losers in the past.

In this strategy, there have been a maximum of 6 consecutive losers in the past with a $4,662.50 maximum drawdown.

The strategy uses two data series. Data1 is five minutes and data2 is a daily chart. The data settings for this are shown below.

Figure 2-7

The settings for data 1 are shown below.

Figure 2-8

The input settings for this strategy are:

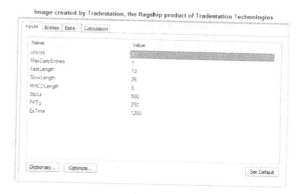

Figure 2-9

Since this strategy uses a daily chart for data2, it is important to do a View, Refresh, Reload on the chart at 6pm EST since the last price on the daily chart is adjusted to the pit close which occurs at 6pm EST. Since the strategy does not trade until 2 am EST. The View, Refresh, Reload can occur anytime between 6pm EST and 2 am EST. Closing the workspace and re-opening the workspace will also cause the price to refresh to the correct value.

This strategy works well back to 7/1/2006, or about 9 years from the time of this writing. The average trade profit is nearly $50 dollar per contract which is a good number for a day trade strategy. Even though we start at 2 am, we still consider this a day trade strategy since we exit by noon CST.

31

The time based inputs for this strategy are based on EST (New York time zone). If your computer is in a different time zone, then you will need to adjust your time zone based on your difference from EST. In this strategy, ExTime is the only time based input.

Since this market trades 24 hours a day, we would not typically consider this type of market for gap fills. When we consider the time of day when there is the most volume and create a custom session, we find this provides us with a window to trade gap fills in the currency futures.

We take a look at some of the latest trades for this strategy in April 2015. Each of these trades hits its profit target. The red vertical lines indicate a session break and a new trading session.

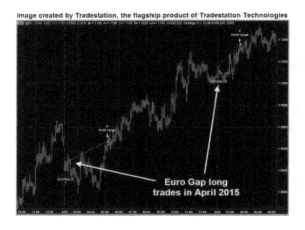

Figure 2-10

32

Setting up Euro Gap in NinjaTrader

Throughout this book, we provide the code and setups for both Tradestation and NinjaTrader. We are able to provide more code screen shots for Tradestation in the book but the NinjaTrader code can be accessed through the website since the code is longer based on the customization that can be made in C#. The instructions for accessing our website are shown in Chapter 16. We like to compare setups and coding in different platforms, using different data feeds. In this section we provide the setup and performance reports for the Gap Fill Euro Currency trading system.

Below are some of the most recent trades in 2015 in the NinjaTrader platform using the Kinetick data feed.

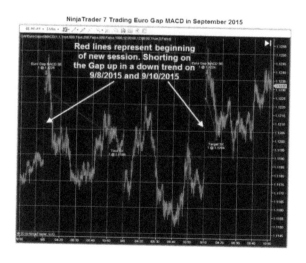

Figure 2-11

The beginning of each session is represented by a red vertical line. Based on our MACD indicator the trend was down so we shorted the gap up. The chart represents a custom session of the European business day from 1am CST to 12 noon CST. We setup the custom session and data settings for this strategy by using the settings shown in the following images.

NinjaTrader 7 Data Settings

⊟ Period	
Price based on	Last
Type	Minute
Value	5
⊟ Chart Style	
Chart style	OHLC
Bar width	1
Color for down bars	Lime
Color for up bars	Lime
⊟ Data	
Load data based on	CustomRange
Start date	7/1/2006
End date	9/22/2015
Session template	EURO MORNING
⊟ Visual	
Auto scale	True
Display in Data Box	True
Label	6E ####-####
Panel	1
Plot session break line	True
Price marker	True
Price marker color	Black
Scale justification	Right
⊞ Session break line	Red; 1px
Show global draw objects	True
⊟ Trades	
Color for executions - buy	Blue
Color for executions - sell	Magenta
⊞ NinjaScript strategy profitable	DarkGreen; 2px
⊞ NinjaScript strategy unprofitab	Crimson; 2px
Plot executions	TextAndMarker

-Figure 2-12

Figure 2-13

The input settings for this strategy in NinjaTrader 7 are shown next.

35

NinjaTrader 7 Euro Gap MACD Strategy Inputs

Debug	
Write debug log	False
Parameters	
01. cntrcts	1
02. MaxDailyEntries	1
03. FastLength	12
04. SlowLength	26
05. MACDLength	9
06. StpLs	True
07. StpLsAmt	500
08. PrfTg	True
09. PrfTgAmt	250
10. Breakeven	False
11. BreakevenAmt	500
12. DollarTrail	False
13. DollarTrailAmt	1000
14. LongExTime	12:00:00
15. ShortExTime	12:00:00
16. CancelReplaceProfitTargetToMarket	True
17. CancelReplaceProfitTargetToMarketSeconds	3
General	
Account	Sim 101
Calculate on bar close	True
	True
Input series	6E 00-00 (5 Min)
Label	CAPEuroGap5MACD
Maximum bars look back	TwoHundredFiftySix
Min. bars required	0
Historical Fill Processing	
Fill type	LiberalWithOpen
Slippage	0
Order Handling	
Entries per direction	1
Entry handling	UniqueEntries
Exit on close	True
Exit on close seconds	30
Stop & target submission	PerEntryExecution
Sync account position	False
Order Properties	
Set order quantity	by strategy
Time in force	Day

Figure 2-14

Next we take a look at the NinjaTrader Performance reports. We like to look at the results in Currency instead of Percentage so that we can see the Average Trade Profit. The most recent performance in 2015 has been down. There are times when Gap Continuations can work better than Gap Fills.

Euro Gap MACD in NinjaTrader 7

Performance	All Trades	Long Trades	Short Trades
Total Net Profit	$44437.50	$7437.50	$37000.00
Gross Profit	$253826.50	$114862.50	$139[illegible]
Gross Loss	$-209387.50	[illegible]	[illegible]
Commission	$0.00	$0.00	$0.00
Profit Factor	1.21	1.07	1.36
Cumulative Profit	$44437.50	$7437.50	$37000.00
Max. Drawdown	$-11912.50	$-14850.00	[illegible]
Sharpe Ratio	0.34	0.05	0.24
Start Date	7/2/2006		
End Date	9/23/2015		
Total # of Trades	1170	574	596
Percent Profitable	60.34%	59.41%	61.24%
# of Winning Trades	706	341	365
# of Losing Trades	464	233	231
Average Trade	$37.98	$12.96	$62.08
Average Winning Trade	$359.50	$332.13	$380.45
Average Losing Trade	[illegible]	$-453.48	$-448.76
Ratio avg. Win / avg. Loss	0.80	0.73	0.86
Max. consec. Winners	10	9	10
Max. consec. Losers	6	6	5
Largest Winning Trade	$4500.00	$2137.50	$4500.00
Largest Losing Trade	[illegible]	[illegible]	[illegible]
# of Trades per Day	0.35	0.17	0.18
Avg. Time in Market	253.6 min	248.1 min	258.1 min
Avg. Bars in Trade	[illegible]	50.6	50.9
Profit per Month	$402.54	$67.36	$338.16
Max. Time to Recover	797.14 days	1382.18 days	456.97 days
Average MAE	[illegible]	[illegible]	[illegible]
Average MFE	$216.94	$200.08	$232.59
Average ETD	[illegible]	[illegible]	[illegible]

Figure 2-15

Euro Gap MACD in NinjaTrader 7

Figure 2-16

As previously mentioned the code and setups for both platforms can be accessed through our website. To learn how to access the website and get the code, see Chapter 16.

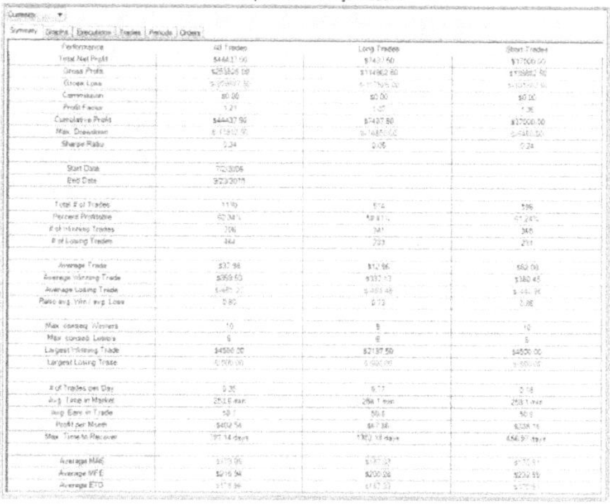

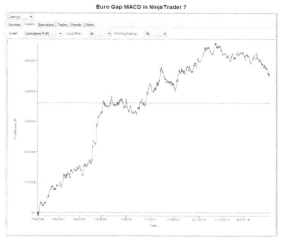

3. Gap Fills in the German Bund

Trading European markets such as the German Bund can provide portfolio diversity for a trading system portfolio. The Eurex financial futures markets in Germany are ideal for trading gap strategies. These markets open each day at 2 am EST and close at 4pm EST. During the week, the Eurex financial futures markets are closed for 10 hours with no after hours or "overnight" session. Any news events or trading perceptions that change during those 10 hours that these markets are closed can provide volatility and new trends when this market opens for traders who need to adjust their position right at the open when volume hits the market.

The US financial futures trade virtually 24 hours per day during the week so any news events that occur can move the US financial futures markets while the Eurex financial futures are closed. The Sydney Futures Exchange begins the global trading day followed by the Asian financial markets. Any news or events in these markets can move the opening prices for the Bunds, Bobl, Schatz (European interest rate futures) and the DAX (European stock index futures) markets in Europe once they open. The news flows out of Europe, becomes the center of attention, once Europe begins its business day, and may change the direction of any opening price movements.

We use a very basic long only Gap Fill strategy to trade German Bunds.

The Strategy

In this section we will begin to develop the strategy by listing the rules for the trade setups.

For Long Entries:

1.) If it is the first bar of the new session and the Open of the first bar of this session is less than the Close of the previous session and is greater than the Close of the previous session minus 0.10 then we go long on the next bar with a market order.

2.) This is a long only strategy that trades on 1 minute bars.

3.) The Stop Loss is 300 Euros and the profit target is 200 Euros.

4.) We exit the trade by 6 am EST if still in the trade.

The Tradestation code is below.

Image created by Tradestation, the flagship product of Tradestation Technologies

```
{ ** Copyright (c) 1998-2015 Capstone Trading Systems All rights reserved. ** }

Inputs: cntrcts(1),
        GapSize(.1),
        StpLs(300), PrfTg(200),
        ExTime(600);

If Date<>Date[1]
    and Open<Close[1]
    and Open>Close[1]-GapSize
    Then Buy ("GapFill German Bund") cntrcts contracts Next Bar at market;

SetStopLoss(StpLs);
SetProfitTarget(PrfTg);
If Time = ExTime Then Sell Next Bar at market;
If Time = ExTime Then Buy to Cover Next Bar at market;
SetExitonClose;
```

Figure 3-1

This is a very basic trading system with a 4 hour time window for the trade from 2:00 am EST to 6:00 am EST. We focus on the long side since there has been a multi-year bullish trend in Interest rate futures across the world and the German Bund is no exception.

The stop loss is 300 Euros with a profit target of 200 Euros.

The data and input settings for this strategy are shown next and are screen shots from the Tradestation platform.

Figure 3-2

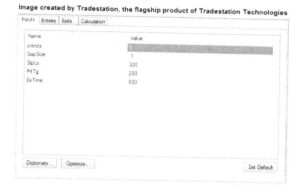

Figure 3-3

One of the most recent trades for this system on September 10, 2015 is shown below.

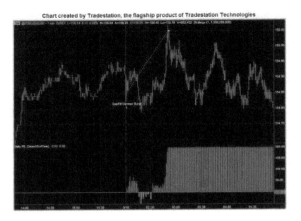

Figure 3-4

We see how the open of the first one minute bar was below the previous day's close and above the previous day's close - 0.10. There is a narrow 10 point range in which we take trades on gap downs. The strategy enters the next bar at the market.

Initially, the price moves against the trade but recovers and the Bund hits its 200 Euro profit target before reversing. This strategy will buy "tight" dips based on the Gap Open. This means that we do not want to go long on a large gap down. Small gaps can more easily continue in the direction of the trend. A move in the direction of the trend is at least a short term reaction based on the trend, even if the market reverses. A larger gap down may be the beginning of some stronger short term selling.

The next image shows the results in the Tradestation Performance Summary in Euros.

42

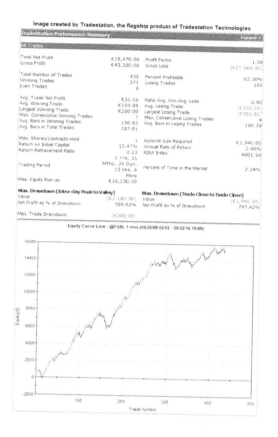

Figure 3-5

We see that the Average Trade Profit is 35.56 Euros since June of 2009. This is about 3.5 ticks in the Bund market. Each 1 tick move in Bunds represents 10 Euros per contract traded. The strategy does not include slippage or commission and works well back to June 2009. The drawdown is 2,180 Euros and is about 62% profitable on 435 trades. The strategy report is shown in Euros.

43

The report can also be displayed in the US Dollar by selecting the Symbol drop down tap at the top. The conversion is done in the Tradestation platform based on the Euro versus US Dollar currency cash value currency conversion for each day. The next report shows us the results in US Dollars.

We see that the average trade profit is $47 dollars with a maximum drawdown of $3,076.

Image created by Tradestation, the flagship product of Tradestation Technologies

TradeStation Performance Summary			Expand ≫
All Trades			
Total Net Profit	$20,590.12	Profit Factor	1.56
Gross Profit	$57,662.75	Gross Loss	($37,072.63)
Total Number of Trades	435	Percent Profitable	62.30%
Winning Trades	271	Losing Trades	156
Even Trades	8		
Avg. Trade Net Profit	$47.33	Ratio Avg. Win:Avg. Loss	0.90
Avg. Winning Trade	$212.78	Avg. Losing Trade	($237.65)
Largest Winning Trade	$300.71	Largest Losing Trade	($448.56)
Max. Consecutive Winning Trades	7	Max. Consecutive Losing Trades	4
Avg. Bars in Winning Trades	136.83	Avg. Bars in Losing Trades	190.39
Avg. Bars in Total Trades	157.81		
Max. Shares/Contracts Held	1	Account Size Required	$2,728.18
Return on Initial Capital	20.59%	Annual Rate of Return	3.12%
Return Retracement Ratio	0.23	RINA Index	4771.38
Trading Period	5 Yrs, 11 Mths, 26 Dys, 13 Hrs, 6 Mins	Percent of Time in the Market	2.24%
Max. Equity Run-up	$21,560.79		
Max. Drawdown (Intra-day Peak to Valley)		Max. Drawdown (Trade Close to Trade Close)	
Value	($3,076.33)	Value	($2,728.18)
Net Profit as % of Drawdown	669.31%	Net Profit as % of Drawdown	754.72%
Max. Trade Drawdown	($448.56)		

Equity Curve Line - @FGBL 1 min.(05/26/09 02:02 - 05/22/15 16:00)

Figure 3-6

When trading a futures market on a non-US exchange, part of your US Dollar account will be converted to the base currency of the market you are trading in order to cover the margin. This is a day trade strategy so your account can be converted back to US Dollars by the end of the day and any currency exchange risk will be very small.

One of the considerations of this strategy when trading in the future is the bias of being long only. The strategy does not work well on the short side but if interest rates move higher (meaning bond prices move lower) then shorting gap ups could become a profitable strategy. Buying gap downs could still be a profitable strategy in a rising interest rate environment (as bond prices fall) since there can be two sided price action when long term trends begin to change.

In chapters 2 and 3 we have covered Gap Fills in both the Euro Currency futures and the German Bund. This is more advanced than an equity or day session stock index futures approach. Discovering gaps in a 24 hour market such as the Euro Currency is based on custom sessions for different time zones. This approach can be applied to other 24 hour currency markets. In this chapter we took a look at trading a foreign futures market such as the Bund. Trading futures and especially foreign futures can sound complex and exotic but once you learn these basic markets, it can become very routine to trade futures markets around the world and provide diversity to your trading portfolio.

Setting Up Gap Fill German Bund in NinjaTrader

In this next section, we setup Gap Fill German Bund in NinjaTrader 7 using the Kinetick data feed. Running this strategy in real time will require real time quotes on the Eurex exchange. Next we show some of the most recent trades in 2015.

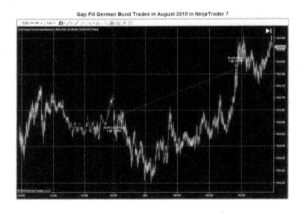

Figure 3-7

The beginning of each session is represented by a red vertical line. We setup the custom session and data settings for this strategy by using the settings shown in the following images.

Figure 3-8

Figure 3-9

47

The input settings for this strategy in NinjaTrader 7 are shown next.

Figure 3-10

The results in NinjaTrader are based on the local currency. For Gap Fill German Bund, the results shown are in the Euro Currency. For all Eurex strategies, the results will be shown in the Euro Currency. Using the Currency drop down tab instead of Percentage, we can see the Average Trade Profit is 36.58 Euros with 71% of trades being profitable.

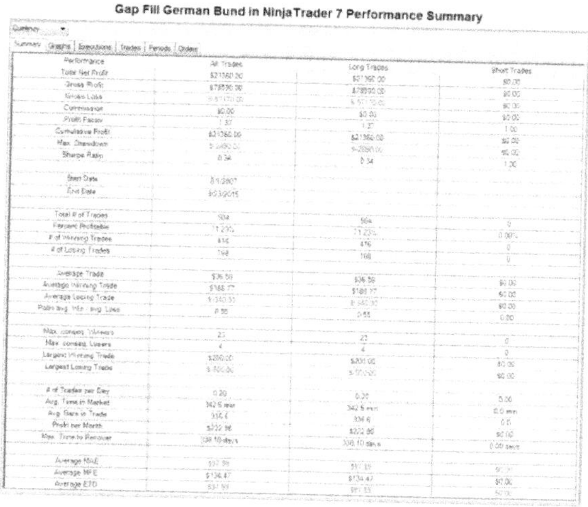

Gap Fill German Bund in NinjaTrader 7 Performance Summary
Summary
Graphs
Executions
Trades
Periods
Orders

Performance	All Trades	Long Trades	Short Trades
Total Net Profit	$21360.00	$21360.00	$0.00
Gross Profit	$78530.00	$78530.00	$0.00
Gross Loss	$-57170.00	$-57170.00	$0.00
Commission	$0.00	$0.00	$0.00
Profit Factor	1.37	1.37	1.00
Cumulative Profit	$21360.00	$21360.00	$0.00
Max. Drawdown	$-2890.00	$-2890.00	$0.00
Sharpe Ratio	0.34	0.34	1.00
Start Date	8/1/2007		
End Date	9/03/2015		
Total # of Trades	584	584	0
Percent Profitable	71.23%	71.23%	0.00%
# of Winning Trades	416	416	0
# of Losing Trades	168	168	0
Average Trade	$36.58	$36.58	$0.00
Average Winning Trade	$188.77	$188.77	$0.00
Average Losing Trade	$-340.30	$-340.30	$0.00
Ratio avg. Win / avg. Loss	0.55	0.55	0.00
Max. conseq. Winners	23	22	0
Max. conseq. Losers	4	4	0
Largest Winning Trade	$200.00	$200.00	$0.00
Largest Losing Trade	$-500.00	$-500.00	$0.00
# of Trades per Day	0.20	0.20	0.00
Avg. Time in Market	342.5 min	342.5 min	0.0 min
Avg. Bars in Trade	334.6	334.6	0.0
Profit per Month	$232.96	$232.96	$0.00
Max. Time to Recover	338.10 days	338.10 days	0.00 days
Average MAE	$97.39	$97.19	$0.00
Average MFE	$134.47	$134.47	$0.00
Average ETD	$97.89	$97.89	$0.00

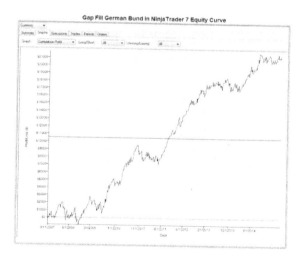

Figure 3-11

Gap Fill German Bund in NinjaTrader 7 Equity Curve

Figure 3-12

See Chapter 16 for instructions on how to download the open code for the strategies.

Gap Fill and Reverse

The Gap Fill and Reverse trading system is an advanced strategy and a continuation of the strategies from our book, "Seven Trading Systems for the S&P Futures". The Gap Fill and Reverse pattern is a frequently occurring pattern and a trade that can be taken after a Gap Fill trade is complete. The Gap Fill and Reverse pattern occurs when the market has a gap open. A gap open occurs when the market opens and there is a price difference from the previous day's close. A gap fill occurs when the market moves from its opening price to the previous day's close. A Gap Fill and Reverse occurs when the market reverses, once the gap fill has occurred and moves back toward the opening price, in the original direction of the opening price of the day.

An example of Gap Fill and Reverse (also known as Gap Fill Fade) price action in the E-mini S&P is shown in the next image.

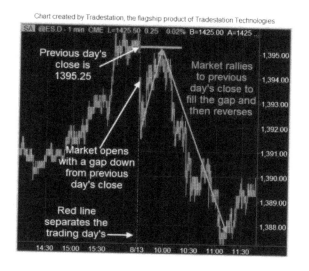

Figure 4-1

This is an example of a gap down in the E-mini S&P futures on August 13, 2012 with a move up in the market to fill the previous day's gap and then a reversal down back to the open to continue in the original direction of the gap. On this particular trading day, the gap down indicated the direction of the trend, so once the trend resumed after filling the gap, the market moved much lower than the original opening prices.

A second example of the Gap Fill and Reverse pattern is demonstrated in the image below on the E-mini Dow futures.

Figure 4-2

This is an example of a gap up on August 19, 2012 with a move down in the market to fill the previous day's gap and then a reversal up to continue in the original direction of the gap. Notice how the market initially rallied and then made new lows on the day before moving higher into the initial direction of the gap up opening price. Patterns don't always instantly respond and sufficient time is needed for trends and strategies to develop.

The Gap Fill and Reverse, which we also reference as a Gap Fill Fade, can be seen as a delayed Gap Continuation pattern where the market will continue in the direction of the gap or initial opening prices after the gap has been filled.

52

Another consideration is the strength of the market. The stronger the trend, the more likely the market may not return to the previous day's close to fill the gap, or if it does, it may only penetrate the previous day's close by a few ticks or less. Penetration of the previous day's close means the amount of points that the market trades lower than the previous day's close on a gap up and the amount of points that the markets trades higher than the previous day's close on a gap down.

Theory

The theory behind a gap fill and reverse (or gap fill fade) is that the original direction of the opening gap indicates the trend based on the overnight price action. The market has a tendency to have quick gap fills during high volatility while lower volatility markets may take some time to fill the gaps. The size of the gap against the trend can also increase the volatility. For example if the trend is up and there is a big gap down or if the trend is down and there is a big gap up, there can be a spike in volatility and price movement in the market.

There can be many reasons for a gap fill to occur. Floor or exchange traders who are flat the market, sensing an oversold market at the open, may quickly buy the gap down to test the weak hands of sellers and create a short covering rally against the weak sellers, creating an accelerated move to the upside. A second scenario is that longer term traders can see a gap down as an opportunity or an entry point to enter into a perceived bullish trend. A third scenario for a buying at the open on a gap downs is when traders with short positions from the previous day's trade choose to take profits at the open forcing the market higher by short covering. Short covering is a way of saying that traders with short positions close their position when buying back the stock or futures contracts for which they have a short position.

A gap fill based on these scenarios can be short lived and the market can turn and move in the original direction of the gap making it a big reversal day that kicks off a multi-day trend. This is the basis for our strategy Gap Fill and Reverse.

Before we develop this strategy, a very active market may follow a fourth scenario. This can be a combination of both the first and third scenario of very active traders or high frequency trading algorithms that tend toward mean reversion. These traders may have short positions at the open based on either having short positions overnight or from the pre-market trade based on news events that may have driven the market down. Many news events happen in the pre-market at 8:30 am EST, one hour before the stock market opens at 9:30 am EST. The high frequency algorithms or active traders that trade these news events one hour before the open and are short at the open, along with the overnight shorts from the previous day's close may not only decide to take profits at the open but to also reverse their position from short to long, buying back their original shorts as well as buying additional contracts to be net long. These same traders could then take profits again, if the market rallies, at any point higher than the open of the day, which was their entry point. The range of the previous day's close +/- 2 points can be a good target for a profit target, depending on how big the original gap is and the current price and value of the market. The previous day's close +/-2 points is also another opportunity to reverse from a long trade to a short trade, for mean reversion back to the open of the day. This would be a very active and ideal scenario that does not always occur in the way described. Sometimes price action goes stale or the market continues at one of these potential turning points without reversing.

In our book, "Seven Trading Systems for the S&P Futures" we discussed how to trade gap fills.

Typically a gap fill trade can be seen as a very short term trade providing us with an opportunity to "fade" the gap once it has been filled. The continuation of the market towards the original gap open, as a reversal from the gap fill, can also be a short term trade testing the original highs or lows of the day, depending on the direction of the gap. If the market gaps up, it will initially be at the high of the day. It can then trade down to the previous day's close to fill the gap. If it reverses, the market may move higher in order to test the original highs made near the open of the day session. If the market gaps down and then reverses and fills the gap by trading higher up to the previous day's close, it could then move back down to test the low of the session that occurred at the open.

In a counter trend or choppy, trendless market environment, the market can move back and forth between these significant points of open, previous day's close, as well as the highs and lows.

If the market becomes trendy, it could then continue to even higher highs from the gap up or lower lows on the gap down if it decides to test those high and low levels.

In this chapter we develop a Gap Fill and Reverse strategy for the E-mini S&P that uses a profit target and takes advantage of the short term nature of the Gap Fill and Reverse pattern.

The Gap Fill and Reverse Strategy using Stop Orders

In this section we will begin to develop the strategy by developing the rules. We will begin by listing the rules for the trade setups.

For Long Entries:

> 1.)   Limit the strategy to one trade per day. There is an input **MaxDailyEntries** so that multiple entries per day can be tested to increase the trading frequency.

2.)   Setup the timeframe to enter trades. We will take trades during the day session between 9:30 am EST until 3:30 pm EST. This timeframe will be setup with inputs so that different timeframes can be tested. The inputs for the timeframe will be **StartTime** and **FinishTime**. We will take trades up until 30 minutes before the day session of the stock market ends at 4:00 pm EST.

3.)   The open must be **greater than the previous day's Close** by at least 2.0 (for the E-mini S&P) as an initial requirement. The **GapSize** input will be used with a default value of 2 so that other values can be tested and other markets can be tested. For example, the Euro Currency may use a value of .001 for 10 pips/points.

4.)   Once the initial requirement is met, the second requirement is that the closing price of the five minute bar must be less than the previous day's close by 2.0 (for the E-mini S&P). The **PenetrationPts** is the input that is used with a default value of 2 to determine how far the market must move below the previous day's close in order for the second entry requirement to be met.

5.)   Once the initial requirements are met as described above in 3 and 4, we place a buy stop at the close of the current five minute bar + PTS (with a default value of .5).

6.)   Once the stop order is filled, we will exit the trade with a Profit Target or a Stop Loss or after we have been in the trade for a pre-defined time. The **Stop Loss, Profit Target**, and **Time to Exit** the trade will also be inputs that can be set to True or False and the values for each can be changed since each value will also have an input. We use a Stop Loss of $650 and a Profit Target of $300. We have additional exit rules in the code such as a Break Even Stop Loss, Dollar Trailing Stop Loss, and Bars Since Entry. By default, these exits are set to false for our example in this chapter but can be researched. In trading, sometimes less is more and too many exit rules can create a strategy that is "over optimized" and will not work as well in the future as it does in the past.

7.)   Since this is a day trade strategy we exit at 4:14 pm EST, or one minute before the futures close. This gives us an opportunity to let profits run as long as possible for a day trade strategy.

For Short Entries:

1.)   Limit the strategy to one trade per day. There is an input **MaxDailyEntries** so that multiple entries per day can be tested to increase the trading frequency.

2.)   Setup the timeframe to enter trades. We will take trades during the day session between 9:30 am EST until 3:30 pm EST. This timeframe will be setup with inputs so that different timeframes can be tested. The inputs for the timeframe will be **StartTime** and **FinishTime**. We will take trades up until 30 minutes before the day session of the stock market ends at 4:00 pm EST.

3.)   The open must be **less than the previous day's Close** by at least 2.0 (for the E-mini S&P) as an initial requirement. The **GapSize** input will be used with a default value of 2 so that other values can be tested and other markets can be tested. For example, the Euro Currency may use a value of .001 for 10 pips/points.

4.)   Once the initial requirement is met, the second requirement is that the closing price of the five minute bar must be greater than the previous day's close by 2.0 (for the E-mini S&P). The **PenetrationPts** is the input that is used with a default value of 2 to determine how far the market must move above the previous day's close in order for the second entry requirement to be met.

5.)   Once the initial requirements are met as described above in 3 and 4, we place a sell short stop at the close of the current five minute bar – PTS (with a default value of
.5).

6.)   Once the stop order is filled, we will exit the trade with a Profit Target or a Stop Loss or after we have been in the trade for a pre-defined time. The **Stop Loss, Profit Target**, and **Time to Exit** the trade will also be inputs that can be set to True or False and the values for each can be changed since each value will also have an input. We use a Stop Loss of $650 and a Profit Target of $300. We have additional exit rules in the code such as a Break Even Stop Loss, Dollar Trailing Stop Loss, and Bars Since Entry. By default, these exits are set to false for our example in this chapter but can be researched. As we mentioned for long entries, when it comes to trading, less is more.

7.)   Since this is a day trade strategy we exit at 4:14 pm EST, or one minute before the futures close. This gives us an opportunity to let profits run as long as possible for a day trade strategy.

For the entries, we like to use the concept of waiting for the price to be below our desired entry point, for longs, (and above our desired entry point for shorts) and then entering the trade using a stop order since it is easier to know there will be a fill if the market hits your price using a stop versus testing a strategy with limit order entries. With the large order book and market depth in the E-mini S&P, we actually get less slippage on stop orders than we do on limit order if we cancel and replace the limit order to a market order. If we don't cancel and replace the limit order to a market order, we may not always get filled. Testing fills based on price trading through the limit order is not exact since you can sometimes get a filled order in real trading when the price does not trade through your limit. This type of fill would not be accounted for in the back test.

We further discuss how to test strategies that use limit orders in Chapter 9.

Another observation to note in this strategy is that the profit target is smaller than the stop loss by a factor of slightly more than two. We use a $650 stop loss versus $300 profit target. This can be the case in a market such as the E-mini S&P where the price action is more counter trend or stop and reverse rather than trend. We may also use the concept of a smaller profit target in comparison to the stop loss in trendier markets during periods where there is more of a counter trend price action.

When the stop loss is larger than the profit target, the percentage profitability must be higher than 50% for the strategy to be profitable. In this strategy, we see that the percentage profitability is around 65%. Many traders prefer to have a reward to risk ratio much higher. My perspective is that a diverse set of strategies using different risk to reward ratios and percentage profitability factors is good for portfolio diversification. It usually requires a trendy market with good range in order for strategies with high reward to risk ratios to be profitable. If a strategy has a profitable hypothetical back test, while the risk is within my risk tolerance, and it helps diversify my portfolio of strategies by working well when other strategies are going through a drawdown, then I will consider using the trading system.

When using only strategies that require big moves so that the reward is higher than the risk, it can be more difficult to trade during pro-longed choppy market conditions. This is an example of the type of strategy that is not correlated with traditional trend based strategies.

Programming the Code

Below we list the code for the Tradestation Platform. The details of the code are valuable for traders who wish to customize or change the code. There are many different options for customizing this code. For example, the strategy can be divided into different inputs for longs and shorts, the GapSize and PenetrationPts could be based on a percentage of the daily range, price, or other market parameters that account for changing market conditions.

```
EasyLanguage Code in Tradestation, the flagship product of Tradestation Technologies
1 // ** Copyright (c) 1998-2015 Capstone Trading Systems All rights reserved. **
2 // Gap Fill Reverse (aka Gap Fill Fade) trading system

4 Inputs: cntrcts(1),
5     GapSize(2), PenetrationPts(2),
6     PTS(.5), MaxDailyEntries(1),
7     StartTime(930), FinishTime(1530),
8     StpLs(True), StpLsAmt(650),
9     PrfTg(True), PrfTgAmt(300),
10    BreakEven(False), BreakEvenAmt(500),
11    DollarTrail(False), DollarTrailAmt(1000),
12    BarsSinceEntryExitLongs(False), BarsToExitLongs(60),
13    BarsSinceEntryExitShorts(False), BarsToExitShorts(60),
14    LongExTime(1610), ShortExTime(1610), ExOnClose(True);
15
16 Vars: Tim(0), Op(0), Cl(0);
17
18 If Date<>Date[1] Then Tim=Time;
19 If Date<>Date[1] Then Op=Open;
20 If Date<>Date[1] Then Cl=Close[1];
21
22 If Time>StartTime and Time<FinishTime
23     and EntriesToday(Date)<MaxDailyEntries
24     and Op>Cl+GapSize
25     and Close< Cl-PenetrationPts
26     Then Buy ("Gap Fill Rev LE") cntrcts contracts
27         Next Bar at Close + PTS Stop;
28
29 If Time>StartTime and Time<FinishTime
30     and EntriesToday(Date)<MaxDailyEntries
31     and Op<Cl-GapSize
32     and Close> Cl + PenetrationPts
33     Then Sell Short ("Gap Fill Rev SE") cntrcts contracts
34         Next Bar at Close - PTS Stop;
35
36 If ExOnClose=True Then SetExitonClose;
37 If Time>LongExTime Then Sell Next Bar at market;
38 If Time>ShortExTime Then Buy to Cover Next Bar at market;
39
40 SetStopContract;
41 If StpLs=True Then SetStopLoss(StpLsAmt);
42 If PrfTg=True Then SetProfitTarget(PrfTgAmt);
43 If DollarTrail=True Then SetDollarTrailing(DollarTrailAmt);
44 If Breakeven=True Then SetBreakEven(BreakEvenAmt);
45
46 If BarsSinceEntryExitLongs=True
47     and BarsSinceEntry(0)>BarsToExitLongs
48     Then Sell This Bar on Close;
49
50 If BarsSinceEntryExitShorts=True
51     and BarsSinceEntry(0)>BarsToExitShorts
52     Then Buy to Cover This Bar on Close;
```

Figure 4-3

Setting up the Chart and Strategy

To set up the chart, we use a continuous contract in the Tradestation platform that only includes the day session data.

63

The symbol for this in the E-mini S&P is @ES.D. The .D extension will only plot the day session data. If @ES is used, the 24 hour session will be plotted. For many of our strategies we use the day session only. For some symbols such as Crude Oil the .D extension is not available so we create custom sessions. We discussed the concept of custom sessions in **Chapter 2.**

To set up the strategy, create a five minute chart of the @ES.D contract going back to 10/1/2001 using the following settings. It might take some time to load this much data if it is the first time loading five minute data back to 2001 for the E-mini S&P.

Figure 4-4

64

Next, Insert the strategy by selecting Insert⌐ Strategy from the menu and then select the strategy name that it was saved as (or compiled as if the code was typed in directly from the previous pages or changed from customization). The strategies default inputs for the E-mini S&P are listed below.

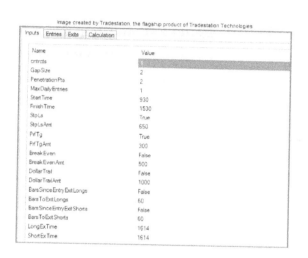

Image created by Tradestation the flagship product of Tradestation Technologies

Name	Value
cntrcts	1
Gap Size	2
Penetration Pts	2
Max Daily Entries	1
Start Time	930
Finish Time	1530
Stp Ls	True
Stp Ls Amt	650
Prf Tg	True
Prf Tg Amt	300
Break Even	False
Break Even Amt	500
Dollar Trail	False
Dollar Trail Amt	1000
Bars Since Entry Exit Longs	False
Bars To Exit Longs	60
Bars Since Entry Exit Shorts	False
Bars To Exit Shorts	60
Long Ex Time	1614
Short Ex Time	1614

Figure 4-5

Input Descriptions

cntrcts = 1 is the default number of contracts. Increase this number to increase the number of contracts.

GapSize = 2 is the default Gap Size from the open to the previous day's close. There must be a gap greater than the GapSize input in order for there to be a trade setup. In this case the GapSize is 2. The current day's open must be greater than the previous day's Close + 2 for a potential long entry or the current day's open must be less than the previous day's Close - 2 for a potential short entry.

PenetrationPts = 2 is the default Penetration points. The penetration points refers to the distance that the gap is penetrated. For example, if the GapSize criteria is met and today's Open is greater than the previous day's close by 2.0 and the current closing price of a five minute bar is less than the previous day's close minus the PenetrationPts value then we place a stop order at the close of the five minute bar + .5. For example, a long trade scenario would be, if the E-mini S&P closes at 1550.00 and the next day, it opens at 1552.25, then moves lower and the close of a five minute bar is less than 1448.00, at 1447.75, a stop order to go long is placed at 1548.25.

A short trade example would be, if the market opens at 1547.00 and the previous day's close was at 1550.00, and the PenetrationPts value is 2.00 and the market moves higher and a five minute close occurs at 1552.25 or higher, (for example 1553.00) then a sell short stop order is placed at the five minute close - .5 (for example, 1552.50).

MaxDailyEntries = 1 is the default number of the maximum daily entries allowed by the strategy.

StartTime = the time to begin taking long or short entries. The default value is 9:30 am EST or the very beginning of the day session.

FinishTime = the time to stop taking long or short entries. The default value is 15:30 pm EST and 30 minute before the stock market closes.

StpLs = True is the default setting for using a stop loss. Set to False to turn off the Stop Loss.

StpLsAmt = The size of the stop loss.

PrfTg = True is the default setting for using a profit target. Set to False to turn off the Profit Target.

PrfTgAmt = The size of the profit target.

BreakEven = False is the default setting for using a breakeven stop loss. Set to True to turn on the Breakeven Stop Loss.

BreakEvenAmt = The size of the break even stop loss.

DollarTrail = False is the default setting for using a dollar trailing stop loss. Set to True to turn on the DollarTrail stop loss.

DollarTrailAmt = The size of the dollar trailing stop loss.

67

BarsSinceEntryExitLongs = True is the default setting for using a Bars Since Entry Exit for Long time exit. In this strategy we are using one minute bars and for the E-mini S&P, the default is True with the BarsToExitLong set to 60 which is 300 minutes.

BarsToExitLongs = The number of bars the strategy will exit a trade if BarsSinceEntryExitLong is set to True.

BarsSinceEntryExitShorts = False is default setting for using a Bars Since Entry Exit for Short time exit. When setting this to True the BarsToExitShorts is the number of bars in which the strategy will exit short trades.

BarsToExitLongs = The number of bars the strategy will exit at trade if the BarsSinceEntryExitShorts is set to True.

LongExTime = 1614 is the default exit time to exit long trades. 1614 is 4:14 pm EST. Time inputs will need to be adjusted to the time zone of the computer where automation is setup.

ShortExTime = 1614 is the default exit time to exit short trades. 1614 is 4:14 pm EST. Time inputs will need to be adjusted to the time zone of the computer where automation is setup.

Setting Up Automation

To setup automation in Tradestation, the symbol will need to be changed to the front month symbol. @ES.D is used in our research and is the default symbol that we use to test and do research.

When we automate the strategy, we change the symbol to the front month symbol. To do this we add the month and the year after the base symbol. The base symbol is @ES. To add the month, we select from one of the 4 following month codes for the E-mini S&P. H=March, M=June, U=September, Z=December. The financials "rollover" four times per year and use these month codes. Other markets like Crude Oil roll over every month and use all 12 month codes for futures rollover.

Next we add the year code for the front month contract. As we write this in May 2015, the front month symbol to use is @ESM15.D. We can also use ESM15.D but we prefer to use the @ symbol to add the back-adjusted contracts in case we need more data for our strategy calculations. If ESM15.D is used right at the time of rollover and 10 days worth of data is needed the ESM15.D data could be "spotty" or "gappy" before the rollover since most of the trading volume is on the front month contracts.

Once the symbol has been changed to @ESM15.D we then turn automation on by going to the top of the menu and selecting Format/Strategy. The following shows the recommended automation settings. We also use the recommended back testing and automation settings in the Backtesting and Automation tabs that we discussed earlier in this chapter.

Figure 4-6

For a complete discussion on the back testing and automation settings, please see Chapter 9.

The historical back test going back to 10/1/2001 without slippage or commission should look like the following Tradestation Performance Summary. The average trade profit is $49.59, the percentage profitability is at 64.62%, and the drawdown is low a $3,575.

70

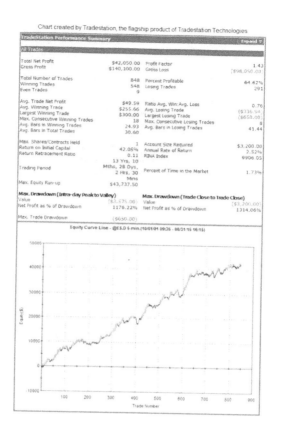

Chart created by Tradestation, the flagship product of Tradestation Technologies

Figure 4-7

This strategy works well going back almost 14 years and after 9/11/2001. After the terrorist attack on 9/11/2001, there were some changes in market structure. The strategy highlights a pattern that has worked since 9/11.

71

Figure 4-8

Setting up the strategy in NinjaTrader

This strategy also works well in the NinjaTrader platform. We show the setup below in NinjaTrader 7 using Kinetick data. The historical data goes back to 9/5/2015 so the comparison with the Tradestation results will be different based on the historical length of the data. We are also using a different programming language. We use C# for this strategy. C# is more explicit and allows us to customize our own order handling. Because of this, there are more details as well as the ability to apply greater customization.

We will first show the data settings. We use a five minute chart of the E-mini S&P with the CME US Index Futures RTH (Regular Trading Hours) custom session that is included with the NinjaTrader 7 platform. The Visual and Trades section of the settings can be set to your personal preferences and do not change the results of the strategy.

Figure 4-9

Figure 4-10

Next we include the input settings which are also the automation settings in NinjaTrader 7. We have some additional

73

inputs so that we define the first bar end time at 9:35 am EST and the last bar end time at 4:15 pm EST. There is also CancelReplaceProfitTargetToMarket inputs with the number of seconds. This is for the profit target. We enter on a stop but use a profit target so that when profit targets are hit, we can cancel and replace the limit order to a market order after a pre-determined number of seconds usually between 0 and 3 seconds, to make sure that we get filled. This would be determined on how we back tested the strategy. We have added an additional fill type called LiberalWithOpen that will show fills on limit orders if the price touches our limit order price instead of requiring it to trade through based on the Default Fill Type. If we use the Default Fill Type then we will hold the limit orders and not Cancel and replace the limit order to the market. If we use the LiberalWithOpen fill type during back testing then we will want to cancel and replace the limit order to a market order. We discuss this in greater detail in Chapter 9.

The NinjaScript also uses .NET functionality so that regardless of your time zone, the time based inputs do not have to be adjusted. The default time based inputs should work regardless of your computer's time zone settings.

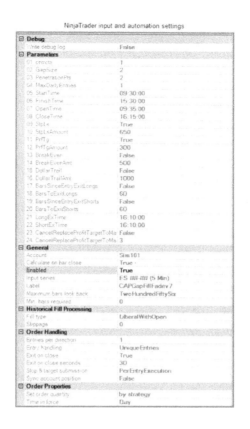

NinjaTrader input and automation settings

⊟ Debug	
Write debug log	False
⊟ Parameters	
01. cntrcts	1
02. GapSize	2
03. PenetrationPts	2
04. MaxDailyEntries	1
05. StartTime	09:30:00
06. FinishTime	15:30:00
07. OpenTime	09:35:00
08. CloseTime	16:15:00
09. StpLs	True
10. StpLsAmount	650
11. PrfTg	True
12. PrfTgAmount	300
13. BreakEven	False
14. BreakEvenAmt	500
15. DollarTrail	False
16. DollarTrailAmt	1000
17. BarsSinceEntryExitLongs	False
18. BarsToExitLongs	60
19. BarsSinceEntryExitShorts	False
20. BarsToExitShorts	60
21. LongExTime	16:10:00
22. ShortExTime	16:10:00
23. CancelReplaceProfitTargetToMa	False
24. CancelReplaceProfitTargetToMa	3
⊟ General	
Account	Sim101
Calculate on bar close	True
Enabled	**True**
Input series	ES ###-### (5 Min)
Label	CAPGapFillFadev7
Maximum bars look back	TwoHundredFiftySix
Min. bars required	0
⊟ Historical Fill Processing	
Fill type	LiberalWithOpen
Slippage	0
⊟ Order Handling	
Entries per direction	1
Entry handling	UniqueEntries
Exit on close	True
Exit on close seconds	30
Stop & target submission	PerEntryExecution
Sync account position	False
⊟ Order Properties	
Set order quantity	by strategy
Time in force	Day

Figure 4-11

Next we show the performance results using the settings above. Keep in mind that the Kinetick data feed that is used goes back to 9/15/2005.

75

Gap Fill and Reverse Trading System Performance Summary Statistics in NinjaTrader 7

Currency | Summary | Graphs | Executions | Trades | Periods | Orders

Performance	All Trades	Long Trades	Short Trades
Total Net Profit	$32975.00	$20487.50	$12487.50
Gross Profit	$105462.50	$63100.00	$42362.50
Gross Loss	$-72487.50	$-42612.50	$-29875.00
Commission	$0.00	$0.00	$0.00
Profit Factor	1.45	1.48	1.42
Cumulative Profit	$32975.00	$20487.50	$12487.50
Max. Drawdown	$-2125.00	$-2562.50	$-2625.50
Sharpe Ratio	0.32	0.26	0.17
Start Date	1/1/2005		
End Date	9/1/2015		
Total # of Trades	624	350	274
Percent Profitable	66.99%	70.57%	62.41%
# of Winning Trades	418	247	171
# of Losing Trades	206	103	103
Average Trade	$52.84	$58.54	$45.57
Average Winning Trade	$252.30	$255.47	$247.73
Average Losing Trade	$-351.28	$-412.71	$-290.35
Ratio avg. Win / avg. Loss	0.72	0.62	0.85
Max. conseq. Winners	17	11	13
Max. conseq. Losers	8	4	7
Largest Winning Trade	$308.00	$300.00	$306.00
Largest Losing Trade	$-650.00	$-650.00	$-650.00
# of Trades per Day	0.17	0.10	0.08
Avg. Time in Market	142.8 min	143.1 min	142.7 min
Avg. Bars in Trade	28.6	28.6	28.6
Profit per Month	$277.52	$172.96	$105.09
Max. Time to Recover	314.82 days	597.07 days	512.77 days
Average MAE	$255.37	$270.38	$235.04
Average MFE	$215.12	$225.62	$201.64
Average ETD	$162.28	$167.14	$156.07

Figure 4-12

Gap Fill and Reverse Trading System Performance Summary Equity Curve in NinjaTrader 7

Figure 4-13

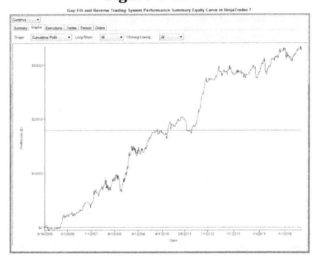

Since 9/5/2015, almost 10 years of data at the time of this writing, this strategy generates 624 trades with 67% profitability and a max drawdown of $3125. The results do not include slippage and commission and use the LiberalWithOpenFill type. The code for this strategy is 734 lines long and is too long to post in this book. The code for this strategy as well as the code for the LiberalWithOpenFill type can be downloaded from our website. See Chapter 16 to get the login details for the website. This is a countertrend trading system and can be used in a portfolio configuration.

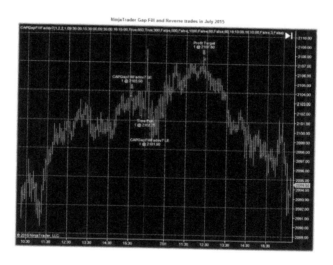

Figure 4-14

5.   Gap Fill and Reverse in the DAX

In Chapter 3, we looked at a Gap Fill strategy in the Bund to expand our trading opportunities to the EUREX. In this chapter we now take a look at the Gap Fill and Reverse that we developed for the E-mini S&P, on the DAX futures. The DAX represents the major stock market index in Germany. The DAX futures have quarterly expirations at the same time as US Stock Index futures. The minimum tick value for the DAX is 12.5 Euros for every ½ point in the DAX.

The DAX has a large daily dollar range and can provide some incredible opportunities. It is typically correlated to the US Stock Index futures even though there has been some divergence from this correlation in 2015. At the beginning of May 2013, we see the Average Daily Dollar Range based on the last 12 days is nearly 3400 Euros. With a big range there is both opportunity and risk. The image below shows a daily chart of the DAX futures. The blue plot at the bottom shows the Average Daily Dollar Range based in Euros. The plot is the Daily High minus the Daily Low (range) multiplied times the point value.

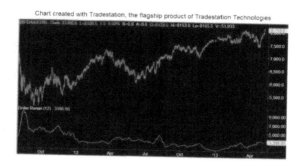

For the DAX, we use the 14 hour session to take a look at the average daily dollar range. In the next image we look at the average daily dollar range of the 24 hour session of the E-mini S&P. We look at the entire session to see the maximum opportunity for the entire session even though this strategy only trades during the day session (9:30 am - 4:00 pm EST) and we define the maximum opportunity as the difference between the high and low of the day, our goal in trading does not include trying to pick exact highs and lows. The measure of the range gives us the maximum opportunity and the larger the range, the larger the opportunity to capture a trend within that range. We also have to realize the increased risk when trading markets with larger daily dollar ranges. Our stop losses typically have to be larger dollar values in these markets so that we do not get stopped out based on the "noise" of the many fluctuations that naturally exist.

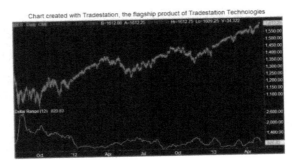

Figure 5-1

The difference in daily dollar ranges between these two indexes is large. The DAX's daily dollar range is more than 5 times larger than the E-mini S&P. We multiply the 3400 Euro range by the current exchange rate of the Euro vs. USD, currently around 1.3000 (in May 2013), to get $4420 for the DAX, compared to $820 for the E-mini S&P.

The DAX trades between 2 am - 4 pm EST. We can create a custom session so that it will display the same times that the US Stock Index futures trade. The only difference between the DAX and the US Stock index futures, for the US day session, is that the DAX closes at 4:00 pm EST instead of 4:15 pm EST. For strategies that exit trades at the end of the day, the exit time should be at 3:59 pm EST or earlier since the DAX futures do trade an additional 15 minutes after the US stock market. The US stock index futures do trade that additional 15 minutes and

80

can set exit times at 4:14 pm EST or earlier. We can set up the Custom Session in Tradestation as shown in the next image.

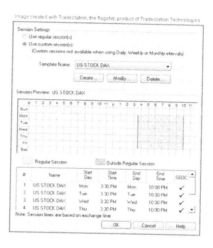

Figure 5-2

The Custom Session times are from 3:30 pm - 10:00 pm since it is based on the Exchange time. The Eurex in Germany is 6 hours ahead of New York and EST. During our fall and spring time changes, there can be some differences when Daylight Savings Time starts between the US and Germany for as long as 3 weeks. This difference can affect the dynamics of this trading system and is one thing that has to be considered when developing trading systems in foreign futures markets. It is not simply a matter of adjusting the time. The dynamics of when these markets open and close relative to the US can change the way these markets function. Back testing strategies during the time period when Daylight Savings Time is not synchronized between the US and Germany will show different performance results.

Since the liquidity and order book are much thinner in the DAX, we use the limit order version of our strategy so that we enter trades using limit orders instead of stop orders. The Tradestation EasyLanguage code for this strategy is shown next.

```
1  // ** Copyright (c) 1999-2016 Capstone Trading Systems All rights reserved. ** ]
2  // Gap Fill Reverse (aka Gap Fill Fade) trading system
3
4  Inputs: cntrts(1),
5      GapSize(1), PenetrationPts(2),
6      MaxDailyEntries(1),
7      StartTime(930), FinishTime(1100),
8      StpLs(True), StpLsAmt(500),
9      PrfTg(True), PrfTgAmt(250),
10     BreakEven(False), BreakEvenAmt(500),
11     DollarTrail(False), DollarTrailAmt(1000),
12     BarsSinceEntryExitLongs(True), BarsToExitLongs(60),
13     BarsSinceEntryExitShorts(False), BarsToExitShorts(60),
14     LongExTime(1614), ShortExTime(1614);
15
16 Vars: Tim(0), Op(0), Cl(0);
17
18 If Date<>Date[1] Then Tim=Time;
19 If Date<>Date[1] Then Op=Open;
20 If Date<>Date[1] Then Cl=Close[1];
21
22 If Time>StartTime and Time<FinishTime
23     and EntriesToday(Date)<MaxDailyEntries
24     and Op>Cl+GapSize
25     Then Buy ("Gap Fill Reverse LE") cntrts contracts
26         Next Bar at Cl - PenetrationPts Limit;
27
28 If Time>StartTime and Time<FinishTime
29     and EntriesToday(Date)<MaxDailyEntries
30     and Op<Cl-GapSize
31     Then Sell Short ("Gap Fill Reverse SE") cntrts contracts
32         Next Bar at Cl + PenetrationPts Limit;
33
34 SetExitonClose;
35 If Time>=LongExTime Then Sell Next Bar at market;
36 If Time>=ShortExTime Then Buy to Cover Next Bar at market;
37 If Time<LongExTime and Time<ShortExTime Then SetExitonClose;
38
39 SetStopContract;
40 If StpLs=True Then SetStopLoss(StpLsAmt);
41 If PrfTg=True Then SetProfitTarget(PrfTgAmt);
42 If DollarTrail=True Then SetDollarTrailing(DollarTrailAmt);
43 If Breakeven=True Then SetBreakEven(BreakEvenAmt);
44
45 If BarsSinceEntryExitLongs=True
46     and BarsSinceEntry(0)>BarsToExitLongs
47     Then Sell This Bar on Close;
48
49 If BarsSinceEntryExitShorts=True
50     and BarsSinceEntry(0)>BarsToExitShorts
51     Then Buy to Cover This Bar on Close;
```

Figure 5-3

As you can see, the code is different based on the entry using a limit order instead of a stop order. The inputs that we use to trade the Gap Fill and Reverse trading system on the DAX are shown below.

Figure 5-4

With these inputs we can see the results of our strategy below in the Tradestation Performance Summary trading the Gap Fill Reverse strategy on the DAX over the last seven years with the performance shown in Euros.

Figure 5-5

This strategy is a selective strategy that generates about 50 trades per year or one trade per week. The drawdown is very low for a DAX strategy considering the average daily dollar range. Since this strategy uses limit orders to enter trades, those limit orders can be held until filled since it is much easier to get a fill on the DAX. The liquidity is much thinner than the E-mini S&P with single digit bid and ask volumes instead of 100s or

1000s of bids and offers in the E-mini S&P. This will allow us to eliminate slippage on the entry.

Setting up the strategy in NinjaTrader

We follow up with the NinjaTrader 7 setup using Kinetick data going back to 1/1/2008. As we have previously mentioned, there can be slight variations in the results based on different data feeds and programming languages.

We use a one minute chart of the DAX with the US Stock Custom Session. This is a special custom session that must be created based on the Custom Session image.

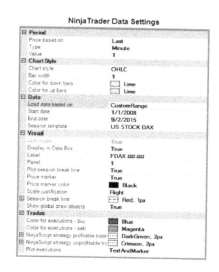

Figure 5-6

85

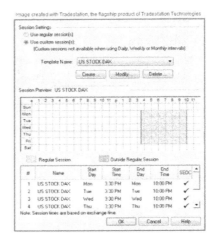

Figure 5-7

Next we include the input settings and automation settings in NinjaTrader. Since this version of the strategy uses a limit order for the entry, we have the input CancelReplaceEntryToMarket. In Chapter 9, we discuss fill types for limit order for back testing and automation.

Figure 5-8

Next we show the performance results using the settings above.

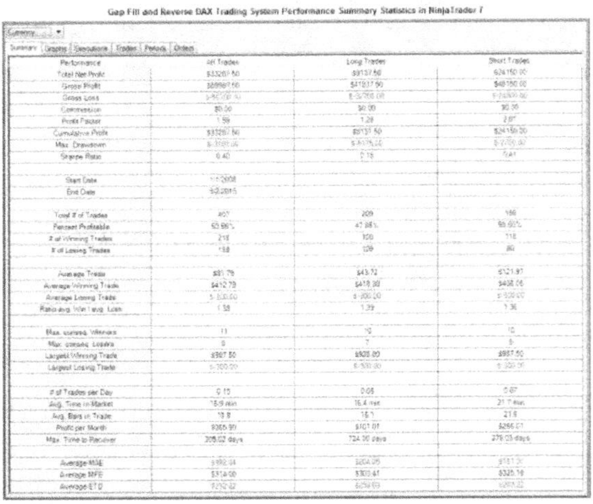

Gap Fill and Reverse DAX Trading System Performance Summary Statistics in NinjaTrader 7

Figure 5-9

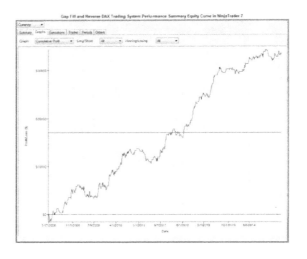

Gap Fill and Reverse DAX Trading System Performance Summary Equity Curve in NinjaTrader 7

Figure 5-10

Since 9/5/2005, almost 10 years of data at the time of this writing, this strategy generates 407 trades with 53% profitability and a max drawdown of $3100. The results do not include slippage and commission and use the LiberalWithOpenFill type. The code can be downloaded from our website.

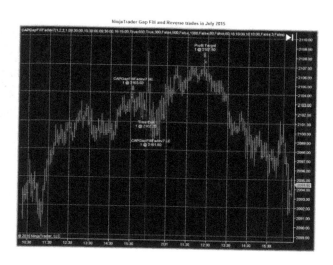

Figure 5-11

The Order Book and Liquidity

We end the chapter by taking a look at a screen shot of the order book. We do this to provide the details of what we mean by liquidity. The liquidity differences can be seen in the matrix screen shots below by observing the difference in sizes of the

89

bids and offers. The first screen shot is a screen shot of the E-mini S&P while the second screen shot is the DAX. The screen shots were taken in the middle of the day on September 4, 2015.

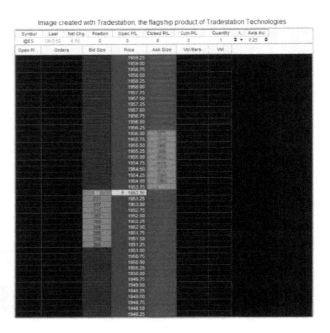

Figure 5-12

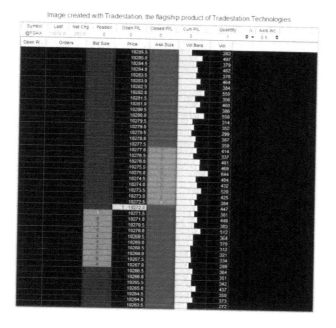

Figure 5-13

If this is your first time to view an order matrix, it allows you to see 10 levels of bids and offers including the bid and offer size at each price 10 levels above the current price for offers and 10 levels below the current price for offers. The bids and offers in the E-mini S&P are 50-100 times greater than in the DAX on average. The advantage of more liquidity is that you can trader more size and will in theory get less slippage on stop and market orders. The disadvantage is that it can be more difficult to get fills on limit orders. We take this into consideration when trading a market and determining if we want to hold limit

91

orders until they are filled or cancelling and replacing limit orders to the market. The bid and offer size can be seen as "standing in line". With more liquidity you can stand in line longer while less liquid markets have a shorter line to wait in. The average daily volume should also be considered since more trades will take place in more popular and more liquid markets. Another observation is that while less liquidity gives us more slippage, markets that are less liquid tend to trend better. I don't want to trade a highly liquid market that has so much liquidity it never moves – similar to a traffic jam.

6.   Gap Fill and Reverse in Crude Oil

Crude Oil is a popular market that we like to trade using both trend and counter trend trading systems. Crude Oil futures can generate some of the most explosive moves and is one of the fastest moving markets to trade. There are strong trends as well as strong reversals. The Gap Fill and Reverse pattern is ideal for Crude Oil. The image below shows a trade on January 28, 2013, for the continuous crude oil futures. At the time of this historical trade analysis, the current contract month was April 2013. Prices have been back adjusted for this trade that would have occurred and would have traded February 2013 Crude Oil.

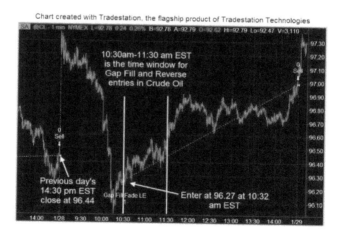

93

Figure 6-1

In Crude Oil we use a narrow time window for entering trades using this reversal pattern between 10:30 am - 11:30 am EST. This window can be extended up until the exit time at 2:29 pm EST. Crude Oil futures pit session closes at 2:30 pm EST and we exit one minute before the pit session closes.

We also use a custom session for this strategy so that prices between 9:00-14:30 EST are shown in the window. The electronic session opens on Sunday at 18:00 EST and closes at Friday at 17:15 EST. Each day at 17:15 pm (starting on Monday) NYMEX Crude Oil closes for 45 minutes until it re-opens at 18:00 EST. When it closes on Friday at 17:15 EST, it then re-opens on Sunday at 18:00 EST. This is virtually a 24 hour market. The open outcry or pit session trades from 9:00 EST to 14:30 EST. This is the reason that we use this timeframe for our custom session.

The following image shows how we set up this custom session in the Tradestation Platform for the Gap Fill and Reverse trading system for Crude Oil.

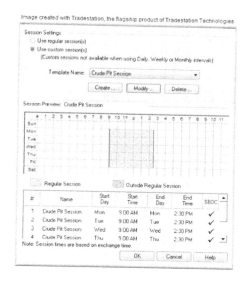

Figure 6-2

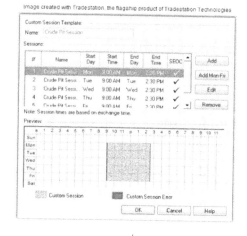

Figure 6-3

95

There can be some big trends in Crude Oil starting early in the day, even before the pit session begins trading at 9:00 am EST. Sometimes trends begin at night when Europe is open while others start between 6-8 am EST. We have observed these trends early in the day and while trends can continue through the entire pit session, research shows the window for reversal patterns related to the Gap Fill and Reverse strategy starts at 10:30 am EST. In a reversal market environment, the initial trend that started in the early morning hours and caused the initial gap (from the previous day's close), has its greatest opportunity to reverse after 10:30 am EST based on research going back to 9/5/2006. We test this strategy back to 9/5/2006 since Crude Oil does not begin trading electronically during the day session until 9/5/2006.

In Crude Oil, we prefer to use limit orders instead of stop orders. We use a Gap Fill and Reverse trading system that is similar to our E-mini S&P Gap Fill and Reverse but slightly different so that we can use limit orders. Even though we are using a different version, we will compare the difference between the two strategies by analyzing the results of how the strategy works with stop orders as well as with limit orders.

Since we are modifying the code for Crude Oil, we will set up the entry rules and then show the Tradestation EasyLanguage code.

The Gap Fill and Reverse Strategy using Limit Orders

In this section we will begin to develop the strategy by developing the rules. We will begin by listing the rules for the trade setups.

For Long Entries:

1.) Limit the strategy to one trade per day. There is an input **MaxDailyEntries** so that multiple entries per day can be tested to increase the trading frequency.

2.) Setup the timeframe to enter trades. We will take trades during the day session between 10:30 am EST until 11:30 pm EST. This timeframe will be setup with inputs so that different timeframes can tested. The inputs for the timeframe will be **StartTime** and **FinishTime**. We will take trades for this one hour timeframe in Crude Oil that has historically shown to generate reversals.

3.) The open at 9 am EST must be **greater than the previous day's Close** at 2:30 pm EST by at least 0.10 (for Crude Oil) as an initial requirement. The **GapSize** input will be used with a default value of 0.10 so that other values can be tested and other markets can be tested. For example, the Euro Currency may use a value of .001 for 10 pips/points.

4.)   Once the initial requirement is met, we can place a limit order to go long at the previous day's 2:30 pm EST Close minus **PenetrationPts** using a default value of 0.10.

5.)   Once the stop order is filled, we will exit the trade with a Stop Loss or one minute before the day session close at 2:29 pm EST since this is a day trade strategy. There are additional exit rules that can be tested but are set to False by default.

For Short Entries:

1.)   Limit the strategy to one trade per day. There is an input **MaxDailyEntries** so that multiple entries per day can be tested to increase the trading frequency.

2.)   Setup the timeframe to enter trades. We will take trades during the day session between 10:30 am EST until 11:30 pm EST. This timeframe will be setup with inputs so that different timeframes can be tested. The inputs for the timeframe will be **StartTime** and

FinishTime. We will take trades for this one hour timeframe in Crude Oil that has historically shown to generate reversals.

3.)   The open at 9 am EST must be **less than the previous day's Close** at 2:30 pm EST by at least 0.10 (for Crude Oil) as an initial requirement. The **GapSize** input will be used with a default value of 0.10 so that other values can be tested and other markets can be tested. For example, the Euro Currency may use a value of .001 for 10 pips/points.

4.)   Once the initial requirement is met, we can place a limit order to go short at the previous day's 2:30 pm EST Close plus **PenetrationPts** using a default value of 0.10.

5.)   Once the stop order is filled, we will exit the trade with a Stop Loss or one minute before the day session close at 2:29 pm EST since this is a day trade strategy. There are additional exit rules that can be tested but are set to False by default.

The EasyLanguage code for this strategy is shown next.

```
1 // ** Copyright (c) 1998-2015 Capstone Trading Systems All rights reserved. **
2 // Gap Fill Reverse (aka Gap Fill Fade) trading system
3
4 Inputs: cntrcts(1),
5     GapSize(.10), PenetrationPts(.10),
6     MaxDailyEntries(1),
7     StartTime(1030), FinishTime(1130),
8     StpLs(True), StpLsAmt(500),
9     PrfTg(False), PrfTgAmt(250),
10    BreakEven(False), BreakEvenAmt(500),
11    DollarTrail(False), DollarTrailAmt(1000),
12    BarsSinceEntryExitLongs(False), BarsToExitLongs(60),
13    BarsSinceEntryExitShorts(False), BarsToExitShorts(60),
14    LongExTime(1429), ShortExTime(1429), ExOnClose(True);
15
16 Vars: Op(0), Cl(C);
17
18 If Date<>Date[1] Then Op=Open;
19 If Date<>Date[1] Then Cl=Close[1];
20
21 If Time>StartTime and Time<FinishTime
22     and EntriesToday(Date)<MaxDailyEntries
23     and Op>Cl+GapSize
24     Then Buy ("Gap Fill Reverse LE") cntrcts contracts
25         Next Bar at Cl - PenetrationPts Limit;
26
27 If Time>StartTime and Time<FinishTime
28     and EntriesToday(Date)<MaxDailyEntries
29     and Op<Cl-GapSize
30     Then Sell Short ("Gap Fill Reverse SE") cntrcts contracts
31         Next Bar at Cl + PenetrationPts Limit;
32
33 If ExOnClose=True Then SetExitonClose;
34 If Time>=LongExTime Then Sell Next Bar at market;
35 If Time>=ShortExTime Then Buy to Cover Next Bar at market;
36
37 SetStopContract;
38 If StpLs=True Then SetStopLoss(StpLsAmt);
39 If PrfTg=True Then SetProfitTarget(PrfTgAmt);
40 If DollarTrail=True Then SetDollarTrailing(DollarTrailAmt);
41 If Breakeven=True Then SetBreakEven(BreakEvenAmt);
42
43 If BarsSinceEntryExitLongs=True
44     and BarsSinceEntry(0)>BarsToExitLongs
45     Then Sell This Bar on Close;
46
47 If BarsSinceEntryExitShorts=True
48     and BarsSinceEntry(0)>BarsToExitShorts
49     Then Buy to Cover This Bar on Close;
```

Figure 6-4

The Tradestation inputs for the limit order version of Gap Fill and Reverse trading system are shown in the next image.

Name	Value
cntrcts	
GapSize	1
PenetrationPts	.1
MaxDailyEntries	1
StartTime	1030
FinishTime	1130
StpLs	True
StpLsAmt	500
PrfTg	False
PrfTgAmt	250
BreakEven	False
BreakEvenAmt	500
DollarTrail	False
DollarTrailAmt	1000
BarsSinceEntryExitLongs	False
BarsToExitLongs	60
BarsSinceEntryExitShorts	False
BarsToExitShorts	60
LongExTime	1429
ShortExTime	1429
ExOnClose	True

Figure 6-5

The point value in Crude Oil is different than in the E-mini S&P so the GapSize is 0.10 (the minimum tick size in Crude Oil is .01) so the gap must be at least 10 ticks from the previous day's close (the close at 14:30 EST) and the limit order is placed 10 ticks or 0.10 (PenetrationPts inputs) on the other side (from the open) of the close.

In the next example we see the entry occurs below the 96.34 price (previous day's close of 96.44 - 0.10 = 96.34) at 96.27 because the timeframe for entry requires that the time must be greater than 10:30. At 10:31 the criteria is met and the trade is entered at 10:32 when the market is 7 points (0.07) below the required
PenetrationPts entry level. The point value is $10 per point or .01 in price movement per contract so the stop loss is placed 50 ticks away or 0.50 from the entry price and we hold the trade until the exit at 14:29 EST.

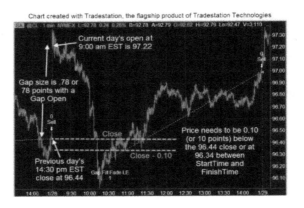

Figure 6-6

The other exit inputs are set to false but could be set to True and tested at different values to customize the strategy. I prefer to use a long term day trade approach to give the strategy time in order to achieve the greatest average trade profit that is possible. This is usually achieved in most trading systems by placing stops $300$800 away from the entry and holding as long as possible to give the strategy room for a big move and then exiting at the close. The stock indexes, low volatility trading periods, or very choppy trading periods are markets and market conditions that can all trade differently and can warrant using profit targets, trailing stop losses, or breakeven stop losses. In general, the more time and "room" a strategy has to "work", then there is a greater opportunity for a higher average trade profit. This has to be balanced with risk and since we are focused on day trade strategies, we exit at the end of the day.

102

Also, a diversity of exits can be used for multi-contract traders by exiting half of your contracts at a set profit target while holding the other half of your contracts until the end of the day to catch a larger move.

We take a look at the Tradestation Performance Summary next. We set the data to go back to 9/5/2006 in the Tradestation Performance Summary since this is the first day that Crude Oil trades electronically during the day session. Before 9/5/2006, Crude Oil did trade electronically but only during the night session. We also do not include slippage or commission in the report but take note of the large average trade profit of $145.51. Limit orders are more easily filled in markets like Crude Oil versus the E-mini S&P.

TradeStation Performance Summary

Expand ⊠

All Trades

Total Net Profit	$90,510.00	Profit Factor	1.56
Gross Profit	$253,410.00	Gross Loss	($162,900.00)
Total Number of Trades	622	Percent Profitable	42.44%
Winning Trades	264	Losing Trades	355
Even Trades	3		
Avg. Trade Net Profit	$145.51	Ratio Avg. Win:Avg. Loss	2.09
Avg. Winning Trade	$959.89	Avg. Losing Trade	($458.87)
Largest Winning Trade	$6,930.00	Largest Losing Trade	($500.00)
Max. Consecutive Winning Trades	7	Max. Consecutive Losing Trades	11
Avg. Bars in Winning Trades	225.53	Avg. Bars in Losing Trades	86.88
Avg. Bars in Total Trades	146.45		
Max. Shares/Contracts Held	1	Account Size Required	$5,940.00
Return on Initial Capital	90.51%	Annual Rate of Return	7.39%
Return Retracement Ratio	0.18	RINA Index	9082.28
Trading Period	8 Yrs, 8 Mths, 19 Dys, 2 Hrs, 58 Mins	Percent of Time in the Market	1.98%
Max. Equity Run-up	$93,690.00		

Max. Drawdown (Intra-day Peak to Valley)		**Max. Drawdown (Trade Close to Trade Close)**	
Value	($6,910.00)	Value	($5,840.00)
Net Profit as % of Drawdown	1309.84%	Net Profit as % of Drawdown	1549.83%
Max. Trade Drawdown	($500.00)		

Equity Curve Line - @CL 1 min.(09/05/06 00:02 - 05/26/15 12:57)

Figure 6-7

We can increase the total net profit and number of trades for this strategy if we extend the Finish Time to one minute before the Exit Time. To do this we set Finish Time, which is the last time a trade entry can take place, to 1428, while the Exit Time is 1429, which is one minute before the pit session close. With an increase in total net profit, there is also an increase of $1610 in drawdown. This increase in drawdown is insignificant

104

for a volatile market like Crude Oil. We do lose about $26 in the average trade profit which amounts to 2.6 points in Crude Oil. There is an increase in number of trades since the window for entries increases from one hour to almost four hours. The Tradestation Performance Summary for this is shown on the next page.

This is an example of how we take a look at a strategy and test different inputs to determine the stability and potential biases of a trading system. Changing one input by a small amount should not "destroy" a system. If this is the case, then we know a system is not stable.

Figure 6-8

We have already shown the input settings for this strategy. Next, we show the data settings that we are using for this strategy setup that are used along with the Custom Session shown at the beginning of this chapter.

Figure 6-9

The Gap Fill and Reverse Strategy using Stop Orders

Next we look at the results of the strategy using stop orders by using the same strategy that we used on the E-mini S&P so that we can compare the results. We also talked about how NYMEX Crude Oil started trading electronically on 9/5/2006 and we have only tested the strategy back to that date. We will test the strategy on pit data prior to 9/5/2006 so that we can see how well the strategy held up on pit data. It was nice to see how well this strategy worked on pit data which was an out of sample test

107

since we developed the strategy from data starting on 9/5/2006 going forward.

To setup the strategy to use stop orders, we use a different EasyLanguage file that uses stop order entries instead of limit order entries. We use the same inputs that we used for the limit order version. The stop order version has one additional input. For the additional input PTS we use .01. In the Stop Order version that we used for the E-mini S&P, we used a hard coded input of .5 instead of PTS. We change our original code that we used for the Emini S&P, to the code shown below so that we have a PTS input that can be changed for different markets or optimized.

```
{ ** Copyright (c) 1998-2013 Capstone Trading Systems All rights reserved. **
  ** Gap Fill Reverse (aka Gap Fill Fade) trading system }

inputs: cntrcts(1),
        GapSize(.1), PenetrationPts(.1), PTS(.01),
        MaxDailyEntries(1),
        StartTime(900), FinishTime(1300),
        StpLs(True), StpLsAmt(500),
        PrfTg(False), PrfTgAmt(900),
        BreakEven(False), BreakEvenAmt(500),
        DollarTrail(False), DollarTrailAmt(1000),
        BarsSinceEntryExitLongs(False), BarsToExitLongs(60),
        BarsSinceEntryExitShorts(False), BarsToExitShorts(60),
        LongExTime(1429), ShortExTime(1429), ExOnClose(True);

Vars: Tim(0), Op(0), Cl(0);

If Date<>Date[1] Then Tim=Time;
If Date<>Date[1] Then Op=Open;
If Date<>Date[1] Then Cl=Close[1];

If Time>StartTime and Time<FinishTime
   and EntriesToday(Date)<MaxDailyEntries
   and Op>Cl+GapSize
   And Close< Cl-PenetrationPts
   Then Buy Next Bar at Close - PTS Stop;

If Time>StartTime and Time<FinishTime
   and EntriesToday(Date)<MaxDailyEntries
   and Op<Cl-GapSize
   And Close> Cl + PenetrationPts
   Then Sell Short Next Bar at Close + PTS Stop;

If ExOnClose=True Then SetExitOnClose;
If Time>LongExTime Then Sell Next Bar at market;
If Time>ShortExTime Then Buy to Cover Next Bar at market;

SetStopContract;
If StpLs=True Then SetStopLoss(StpLsAmt);
If PrfTg=True Then SetProfitTarget(PrfTgAmt);
If DollarTrail=True Then SetDollarTrailing(DollarTrailAmt);
If Breakeven=True Then SetBreakEven(BreakEvenAmt);

If BarsSinceEntryExitLongs=True
   and BarsSinceEntry(0)>BarsToExitLongs
   Then Sell This Bar on Close;

If BarsSinceEntryExitShorts=True
   and BarsSinceEntry(0)>BarsToExitShorts
   Then Buy to Cover This Bar on Close;
```

Figure 6-10

We use the same data settings that we used with the limit order version and the input settings listed below.

109

Image created by Tradestation, the flagship product of Tradestation Technologies

Figure 6-11

The Tradestation Performance Summary is shown below. We see that the results are also profitable and similar to the limit order version. The results are hypothetical and do not include slippage or commission.

110

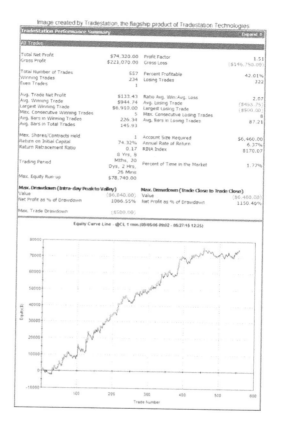

Figure 6-12

We developed this strategy from 9/5/2006 forward since that is when Crude went electronic during the day session. Many times a market can trade differently when it trades electronically instead of when it is only pit traded. We take a look at the limit order version starting on 9/4/2006 going back to January, 1987, the beginning of our Crude Oil data in Tradestation on one minute charts to see how the strategy works on out of sample testing.

111

Using the same data and input settings as the limit order version, we see that there are some really nice results from 9/4/2006 back to 2004. From 2004 back to 1987, there are not as many trades and the equity curve is sideways. This is positive news as there is never a really large drawdown in our out of sample testing. We could probably change the GapSize and PenetrationPts inputs to generate more trades prior to 2004. The Tradestation Performance Summary is shown below.

Figure 6-13

Additionally, we test the basic Gap Fill and Reverse trading system with limit orders on West Texas Intermediate and Brent Crude Oil. In Tradestation, the symbol to use for West Texas Intermediate is @WBS=107XN. The symbol to use for Brent Crude Oil is @BRN=107XN. The data and input settings are the same as those used on Nymex Crude Oil (@CL). The performance results for West Texas Intermediate Crude Oil are shown first, followed by the results for Brent Crude Oil.

In Tradestation you will need the European Region data to run the backrests. With European Region data, you will get delayed data for these markets. To setup automation, you will need to add additional live data to the European region. In many of the symbols in Tradestation such as Crude Oil, there are continuous contract symbols such as @CL. For West Texas Intermediate and Brent Crude Oil, there was not a continuous symbol available at the time of this writing (such as @WTI or @BRN) so we used the custom symbols to create the back adjusted data to test this strategy on these markets.

TradeStation Performance Summary

All Trades

Total Net Profit	$59,230.00	Profit Factor	1.58
Gross Profit	$161,250.00	Gross Loss	($102,020.00)
Total Number of Trades	410	Percent Profitable	44.15%
Winning Trades	181	Losing Trades	228
Even Trades	1		
Avg. Trade Net Profit	$144.46	Ratio Avg. Win:Avg. Loss	1.99
Avg. Winning Trade	$890.88	Avg. Losing Trade	($447.46)
Largest Winning Trade	$4,720.00	Largest Losing Trade	($530.00)
Max. Consecutive Winning Trades	4	Max. Consecutive Losing Trades	7
Avg. Bars in Winning Trades	213.42	Avg. Bars in Losing Trades	88.06
Avg. Bars in Total Trades	143.76		
Max. Shares/Contracts Held	1	Account Size Required	$5,730.00
Return on Initial Capital	59.23%	Annual Rate of Return	6.89%
Return Retracement Ratio	0.22	RINA Index	7523.40
Trading Period	6 Yrs, 9 Mths, 4 Hrs, 39 Mins	Percent of Time in the Market	1.76%
Max. Equity Run-up	$64,260.00		

Max. Drawdown (Intra-day Peak to Valley)		Max. Drawdown (Trade Close to Trade Close)	
Value	($6,100.00)	Value	($5,730.00)
Net Profit as % of Drawdown	970.98%	Net Profit as % of Drawdown	1033.68%
Max. Trade Drawdown	($530.00)		

Equity Curve Line - @WBS+107XN 1 min.(08/25/08 09:01 - 05/27/15 14:30)

Figure 6-14

Figure 6-15

It is positive to see that the strategy works well in out of sample testing as well as on other similar market such as Brent Crude and West Texas Intermediate. You ask the question "Is this optimized?" This is a very basic strategy developed based on market observations. The inputs are very general and are the same on long and short trades. The stop loss is $500. There are no timeframe biases where we change the inputs during

115

different time periods. This is one of my favorite ways to develop a strategy.

That is, by seeing a pattern and testing it on basic inputs without using the optimization tool. Does it mean this strategy will now always work going forward? No, it is not possible to know if it will or if it will not. It gives us a good place to start. Sometimes markets change and patterns no longer work. The best approach would be to trade the strategy if you like the way the strategy works, believe in the approach, and are willing to assume the capital risk of the maximum drawdown and then some if the strategy goes into a worse case drawdown. I say "then some" to account for automation errors or worse case drawdowns. It is best to assume the strategy will have a new maximum drawdown in the future and to determine in advance, how to handle the drawdown.

One of the best ways to prepare for a worse case drawdown is to wait for the strategy to go into at least a small 1k-2k drawdown (or more) from a recent equity peak before starting. This can work as a cushion. Trading a portfolio of diverse trading systems can also help to balance the drawdown cycles and reduce the drawdown so that it is less than the sum of the max drawdown for each system being trading.

Setting up the strategy in NinjaTrader

Next we setup the Gap Fill and Reverse strategy for Crude Oil in NinjaTrader 7 using Kinetick data going back to 9/5/2006. As we have previously mentioned, there can be slight variations in the results based on different data feeds and programming languages.

We use a one minute chart of Crude Oil futures with the NYMEX Energy RTH Custom Session that is already in the NinjaTrader platform.

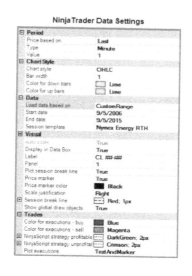

Figure 6-16

NinjaTrader Custom Session

Session template: Nymex Energy RTH

[New...] [Copy...] [Delete]

The selected template contains the following sessions...

Start Day	Start Time	End Day	End Time
Monday	9:00 AM	Monday	2:30 PM
Tuesday	9:00 AM	Tuesday	2:30 PM
Wednesday	9:00 AM	Wednesday	2:30 PM
Thursday	9:00 AM	Thursday	2:30 PM
Friday	9:00 AM	Friday	2:30 PM

[Add...] [Edit...] [Delete]

The sessions above are based on the following time zone...

(UTC-05:00) Eastern Time (US & Canada) (Amex, Arca, Box, Brut ▼)

[OK] [Save] [Cancel]

Figure 6-17

Next we include the input settings and automation settings in NinjaTrader 7. Since this version of the strategy uses a limit order for the entry, we have the input CancelReplaceEntryToMarket. In **Chapter 9 How to Test Trading Systems with Limit Orders**, we discuss the fill types for limit orders used for back testing and automation.

Figure 6-18

Next we show the performance results using the settings above.

Gap Fill and Reverse Crude Oil Trading System with Limit Orders Performance Summary in NinjaTrader 7

Performance	All Trades	Long Trades	Short Trades
Total Net Profit	$55130.00	$24980.00	$30150.00
Gross Profit	$199170.00	$85970.00	$113200.00
Gross Loss	$-144040.00	[illegible]	[illegible]
Commission	$0.00	$0.00	$0.00
Profit Factor	1.38	1.41	1.36
Cumulative Profit	$55130.00	$24980.00	$30150.00
Max. Drawdown	[illegible]	[illegible]	[illegible]
Sharpe Ratio	0.23	0.19	0.15
Start Date	9/5/2006		
End Date	9/9/2015		
Total # of Trades	626	332	294
Percent Profitable	45.37%	51.20%	38.78%
# of Winning Trades	284	170	114
# of Losing Trades	342	162	180
Average Trade	$88.07	$75.24	$102.55
Average Winning Trade	$701.30	$605.71	$982.36
Average Losing Trade	$-421.17	[illegible]	$-461.36
Ratio avg. Win / avg. Loss	1.67	1.34	2.16
Max. consec. Winners	5	6	6
Max. consec. Losers	9	7	8
Largest Winning Trade	$6870.00	$2860.00	$6870.00
Largest Losing Trade	[illegible]	[illegible]	[illegible]
# of Trades per Day	0.19	0.10	0.09
Avg. Time in Market	92.1 min	48.5 min	141.3 min
Avg. Bars in Trade	91.5	48.2	141.2
Profit per Month	$515.00	$234.07	$281.95
Max. Time to Recover	947.87 days	543.95 days	993.35 days
Average MAE	$387.69	[illegible]	[illegible]
Average MFE	$643.50	$513.16	$790.56
Average ETD	[illegible]	[illegible]	[illegible]

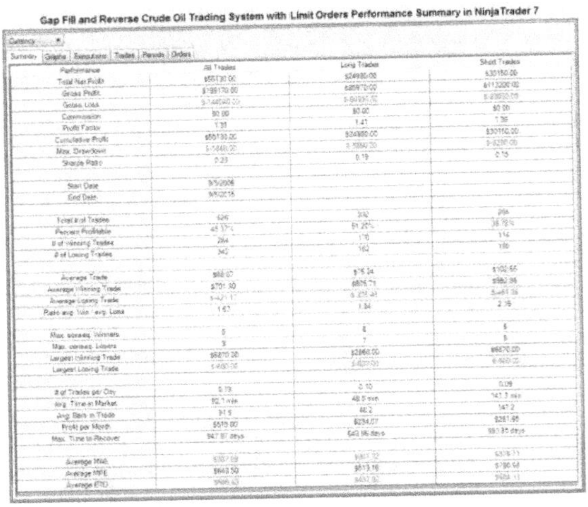

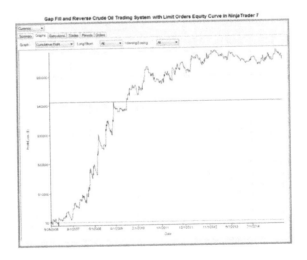

Figure 6-19

Figure 6-20

Since 9/5/2006, almost 10 years of data at the time of this writing, this strategy generates 626 trades with 45% profitability and a max

drawdown of $5,840. The results do not include slippage and commission and use the LiberalWithOpenFill type. The code can be downloaded from our website.

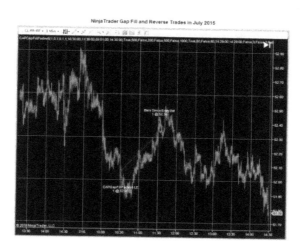

Figure 6-21

7.   Gap Fill and Reverse in the Euro Currency

One of our favorite markets to trade is the Euro Currency futures. Typically this is one of the trendiest markets to trade and provides the best intra-day trends. Recent market activity over the past few years has shown narrower daily ranges and fewer trends in this market. The Gap Fill and Reverse trading system is considered a countertrend trading system. When developing portfolios of trading systems, it can be advantageous to trade both trend and countertrend trading systems in different markets and market sectors such as stock indexes, energies, currencies, bonds, etc. The markets can change between trend and countertrend mode and then back to trend mode, alternating on a daily basis. Markets can also remain very trendy for a long period of time and then transition quickly (or slowly) to a more countertrend market environment. It can be difficult to know which type of strategy to trade on any given day since there is no exact frequency or pattern in which markets change between trend and countertrend. Trading both types of systems can provide diversity for both types of market conditions.

We apply the Gap Fill and Reverse trading system to the Euro Currency using our EURO CRUDE custom session. The Euro Crude Custom session starts when the DAX and Bund open at 2am EST and end when the pit session of Crude Oil closes at 2:30 pm EST.

We use the following inputs for the Euro Gap Fill and Reverse with limit orders.

Figure 7-1

The minimum tick in the Euro is .0001. We require the Gap Size to be 10 points or .0010 while the Penetration Points is on only 4 points or .0004. We start taking trade entries at 7:30 am EST and stop taking trade entries at 12:00 noon EST. All trades are exited at 200 pm EST. This custom session lasts 12.5 hours with the Tradestation setup for the custom session shown below.

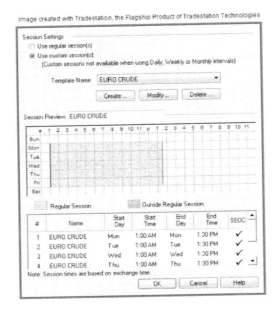

Figure 7-2

Additionally, the data settings for this strategy are shown next.

Figure 7-3

The Euro Currency futures have been traditionally trendy but since 2009 this countertrend trading system has worked well in this market. The Tradestation Performance Summary since 2010 is shown below and does not include slippage or commission. The average trade profit is $68 per contract.

Figure 7-4

Setting up the strategy in NinjaTrader

Next we setup the Gap Fill and Reverse strategy for Crude Oil in NinjaTrader 7 using Kinetick data going back to 9/1/2009. As we have previously mentioned, there can be slight variations in

126

the results based on different data feeds and programming languages.

We use a one minute chart of Crude Oil futures with the Euro Crude Custom Session. The Euro Crude must be created based on the NinjaTrader Custom Session image. This session runs from 9:00 am EST to 2:30 pm EST, Monday through Friday.

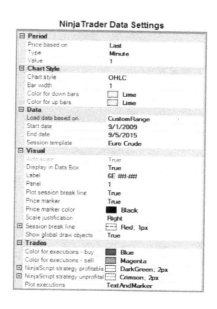

Figure 7-5

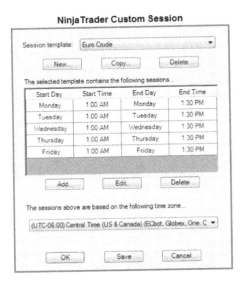

Figure 7-6

Next we include the input settings and automation settings in NinjaTrader 7. Since this version of the strategy uses a limit order for the entry, we have the input CancelReplaceEntryToMarket. In

Chapter 9 How to Test Trading Systems with Limit Orders, we discuss fill types for limit orders for back testing and automation.

128

NinjaTrader Input Settings Gap Fill and Reverse Euro Currency with Limit Orders

Debug	
Write debug log	False
Parameters	
01. cntrcts	1
02. GapSize	0.001
03. PenetrationPts	0.0004
04. MaxDailyEntries	1
05. StartTime	07:30:00
06. FinishTime	12:00:00
07. OpenTime	02:01:00
08. CloseTime	14:30:00
09. StpLs	True
10. StpLsAmount	800
11. PrfTg	True
12. PrfTgAmount	500
13. BreakEven	False
14. BreakEvenAmt	500
15. DollarTrail	False
16. DollarTrailAmt	1000
17. BarsSinceEntryExitLongs	True
18. BarsToExitLongs	60
19. BarsSinceEntryExitShorts	False
20. BarsToExitShorts	60
21. LongExTime	14:00:00
22. ShortExTime	14:00:00
23. CancelReplaceEntryToMarket	False
24. CancelReplaceEntryToMarketSeconds	3
25. CancelReplaceProfitTargetToMarket	False
26. CancelReplaceProfitTargetToMarketSeconds	3
General	
Account	Sim101
Calculate on bar close	True
Enabled	**True**
Input series	6E ###.## (1 Min)
Label	CAPGapFillFadev5
Maximum bars look back	TwoHundredFiftySix
Min. bars required	0
Historical Fill Processing	
Fill type	LiberalWithOpen
Slippage	0
Order Handling	
Entries per direction	1
Entry handling	UniqueEntries
Exit on close	True
Exit on close seconds	30
Stop & target submission	PerEntryExecution
Sync account position	False
Order Properties	
Set order quantity	by strategy
Time in force	Day

Figure 7-7

Next we show the performance results using the settings above.

Gap Fill and Reverse Euro Currency Trading System with Limit Orders Performance Summary in NinjaTrader 7

Performance	All Trades	Long Trades	Short Trades
Total Net Profit	$37,900.00	$21,487.50	$16,412.50
Gross Profit	$130,975.00	$66,750.00	$64,225.00
Gross Loss	-$93,075.00	-$45,262.50	-$47,812.50
Commission	$0.00	$0.00	$0.00
Profit Factor	1.41	1.47	1.34
Cumulative Profit	$37,900.00	$21,487.50	$16,412.50
Max. Drawdown	-$6,731.50	-$5,762.50	-$6,426.50
Sharpe Ratio	0.28	0.29	0.24
Start Date	9/1/2009		
End Date	9/8/2015		
Total # of Trades	585	273	292
Percent Profitable	63.74%	65.57%	61.64%
# of Winning Trades	341	179	162
# of Losing Trades	194	94	100
Average Trade	$72.84	$78.71	$62.64
Average Winning Trade	$384.09	$372.91	$396.45
Average Losing Trade	-$476.77	-$433.52	-$478.13
Ratio avg win / avg loss	0.80	0.77	0.83
Max. consec. Winners	10	12	10
Max. consec. Losers	6	4	7
Largest Winning Trade	$737.50	$675.00	$737.50
Largest Losing Trade	-$987.50	-$450.00	-$450.00
# of Trades per Day	0.24	0.12	0.12
Avg. Time in Market	202.3 min	206.9 min	197.4 min
Avg. Bars in Trade	201.8	206.4	197.0
Profit per Month	$529.04	$299.94	$230.79
Max. Time to Recover	371.35 days	361.15 days	651.30 days
Average MAE	$357.29	$361.91	$385.14
Average MFE	$342.41	$346.85	$338.20
Average ETD	$271.57	$269.34	$273.73

Figure 7-8

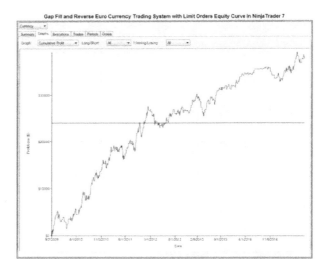

Figure 7-9

130

Since 9/1/2009, this strategy generates 535 trades with 63% profitability and a max drawdown of $4,763. The results do not include slippage and commission and use the LiberalWithOpenFill type. The code can be downloaded from our website at:

http://algorithmictradingsystemscode.com

Next we show an example trade in the NinjaTrader platform. We have kept this chapter very basic as it is the same strategy that we have already applied to other markets. In this chapter we simply applied it to the Euro Currency futures using a custom session.

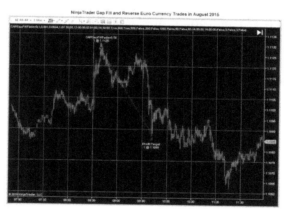

Figure 7-10

131

8.   Important Trading System Principals

In the next five chapters we discuss some of the principles that we apply to trading system development. There is false information and education in the trading world that looks good, is intuitive, and works great on a few cherry picked trades. Many of these principles, and popular Wall Street axioms such as **"You can't go broke taking profits"** and **"Don't let a winning trade turn into a losing trade"** are not completely accurate and are not always interpreted correctly. We challenge these principles and find them to be more of a benefit to your broker than to you since they can cause increased trading frequency and reduced trading profits. It is important to accurately test an idea on market data rather than consider the "seat of the pants" biased math where we convince ourselves that "this type of trade will work".

I speak from experience, having violated many of the rules that do work before realizing the errors in my trading. It is easy to think that because we know the point value of the market that we are trading and because we are good at math, we can look at an intraday chart, see a familiar technical pattern and determine that if we buy x number of futures contracts at price A and then sell them at price B, we will make y amount of dollars and this will put our account up z%.

Creating a mathematical 3:1 reward to risk ratio based on a chart's technical pattern doesn't mean it is a good trade to take. After all, we have no idea what the winning percentage of this popular technical pattern is on this market in this timeframe. What if the technical pattern we observe works only 20% of the time? (Many popular technical analysis patterns have a low percentage of profitability working only 20-30% of the time, but can work very well when they do work and can capture some big moves).

If this popular technical analysis pattern works only 20% of the time and we use a 3:1 reward to risk ratio, meaning our profit target is 3 times larger than our stop loss risk, do we have a positive advantage in this market and on this trade? The answer is NO! Our advantage on this trade is negative. How do we calculate our advantage? We multiply our win ratio by the percentage of time it is profitable and subtract the losing ratio by the percentage of time the strategy is not profitable. The equation for this would look like this:

$$3*20\% - 1*80\% = -0.20$$

Our advantage on this trade is a negative number of -0.20. If we had done our research, we would learn that while this is not necessarily a bad trade based on the technical pattern we observed, it only has a 20% chance of it being profitable. Maybe your first trade was a winner so you thought it was a good strategy. We find out later that it doesn't seem to work anymore or that our account balance is down, when in reality our profit target should be much higher for this trade to work. This would typically indicate a longer holding period in order for us to achieve a winning trade that would hit a larger profit target. We also need to study volatility and range to determine the appropriate size of a stop loss that we would use and if a 5:1 win/loss ratio is feasible in the current market environment depending on range and volatility. If it is, are we willing to risk the right amount for a reasonable stop loss and base that stop loss on the market instead of our account size?

This is a simple theoretical example. When other additional exit rules such as day trade exits, time based exits, trailing stops, and breakeven stops are applied then the analysis is not as straightforward. For day trade strategies, we exit at the end of the day and we may not hit our stop loss or profit target (therefore changing our average win/loss ratio based solely on the profit target to stop loss ratio, without taking into account an end of day exit).

Many traders like to have a strategy where there are a high percentage of winners since this means they are "right", which creates a feeling of success. In the next set of chapters we will take a look at how profit targets can affect trading profits and how a high percentage of winners do not always create trading success. **You can go broke taking profits if your winners are not big enough to offset your losers and transaction costs.** In the next five chapters we show how we test profit targets and stop losses in our trading systems to find the right balance and how to test limit orders in a trading system.

There will be many times when a trading system "looks dumb" because it gives profits back or almost hits its profit target only to see the market reverse and for the trade to get stopped out.

It is important to understand the principles in the following chapters and how important it is to follow them in a trading system, even when they look dumb, instead of micro-managing your trades, only to go broke.

9.   How to Test Trading Systems

with Limit Orders

In this chapter, we discuss the concept of back testing and automating strategies that use limit orders. In the previous chapters our discussions have been based on trading system development. Many of the strategies we have developed use either a limit order on entry and/or a limit order on exit (with a profit target). It is important to understand the limitations in back testing when testing strategies that use limit orders.

Cancelling and Replacing Limit Orders To the Market

When Tradestation back tests a strategy, by default, it reports a fill for a limit order when the historical price touches the price where the limit order is located. We do not know if that order would have been filled in real time trading when testing it this way. To make sure that our real time results match our hypothetical system signals going forward in live trading, we typically cancel and replace limit orders to market orders in live trading so that we make sure that we get an entry on every trade signal since some of the best trades can go immediately in our favor and missing a winning trade will add to our risk since it did not make up for the losing trades that we would naturally incur since all losing trades would eventually get filled. This means we would capture all losing trades but miss some winning trades if we held our limit orders until filled.

We use an average slippage and commission number in our back test to account for the slippage we will get when cancelling and replacing limit orders to the market. This is traditionally the way we test and trade strategies that use limit orders and with our slippage and commission factors that we add to the test, our hypothetical results come very close to real time trading results. More liquid markets such as the E-mini S&P with 1000s of bids and offers at every price can be difficult to get a limit order filled if we wait for a fill. We want to eliminate the scenario where our real time results become out of sync with the trading system signals since the trading system would show the winner but our real account would not show the winning trade because the limit order was not filled and we were stubborn about not taking any slippage. This can be a "penny wise and pound foolish" way to trade since we did not want to give up 1 tick on average to potentially capture a big winner.

The settings that we use to back test and automate strategies for our traditional scenario are shown below with the first image showing the back test settings and the second image showing the automation settings for Tradestation. To get to this menu selection, go to Format Strategies, then Select Properties for All and then Select the Backtesting tab. In the image below, there are two options outlined in the green box. We select the first option in the Backtesting tab as well as the first set of options in the Automation tab.

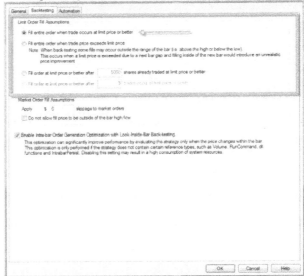

Figure 9-1

138

Figure 9-2

To reiterate, when we setup automation to match the back testing scenario option of "Fill entire order when trade occurs at limit price or better" approach, we will show a fill when back testing if the price touches the limit order, even if the price does not pass through the limit order. The strategy may or may not get filled in real trading in this scenario. It is not possible to know with a back test if the strategy would have been filled in the past. When implementing a strategy with limit orders to match this type of back testing, we setup automation so that we cancel and replace the limit order to a market order within 0 to 3 seconds and then assume we will get slippage since the price will be at the bid when touching the limit order for longs and when we cancel and replace it to a market order, it will get at least 1 tick of slippage up to the offer (based on a long trade). I prefer to assume there will be slippage and to take the slippage and know that I am in the trade rather than trading with the uncertainty of not knowing if my limit order will get filled.

Holding Limit Orders Until they are Filled

There is a way to back test a strategy in Tradestation to determine how well it would work if we held the limit order until there was a fill by asking Tradestation to not report a fill during the back test unless the trade price exceeds where our limit order would be. This means that the strategy testing would not show a fill unless the price traded by at least 1 tick below the limit order price for longs or at least 1 tick above the limit order price for shorts. In the previous section, I said, "This can be a 'penny wise and pound foolish way' to trade" in reference to holding limit orders until they are filled. The key word is "can". If an accurate back test and automation setup can be achieved, then this can be a profitable and correct way to trade. It is more sophisticated and takes more effort to back test and automate a trading system using this approach. We explain how to do this in this section.

As we mentioned in the previous chapter, we discussed the consideration of the type of market and how easy it is to fill limit orders in a particular market. In less liquid markets where there is single digit volume at the bids and offers or typically less than a volume of 20 at the bids and offers, or more volatile or "wiggly" markets, then limit orders can be easier to fill. Examples of this type of market are DAX, Gold, and Crude Oil. If a back test shows good results when holding limit orders until they are filled then this can be a good way to trade that particular market with that particular strategy.

Running a back test on a trading system that holds limit orders until they are filled produces less accurate results of what can be achieved in live trading and can be considered more of a "worse case scenario". The reason that it is a "worse case scenario" is that sometimes in real trading a limit order that is held at the price (instead of cancelling and replacing to the market) will get filled even though the price did not trade through limit order. In this case, your entry was at a short term low for longs or a short term high for shorts and would end up being a profitable trade that was included in real time trading but would not show up on a back test since price did not trade through the limit. Automation of a strategy with this setting can be out of sync with the trading system when using our traditional automation settings since a real world fill can occur but the strategy does not show it as filled if the market did not trade by at least 1 tick past the limit order. There is a way to set up automation so that it will be in sync with the strategy and we will discuss how to set this up.

Typically the back test results will be worse than real world trading results when back testing using the "Fill entire order when trade price exceeds limit price" option since it is a worst case scenario since and it will miss some winning trades in the back test that actually get picked up in live trading. The amount of slippage and commission used in the previous scenario where we Cancel and Replace Limit Orders to the market can be reduced in this scenario where we require price to trade through the limit in order to get filled. We will still have to account for slippage on stop orders. Because of this, we can typically cut the slippage calculation we used in the first scenario in half for a strategy that has 50% winners. We also have to consider if we use a time exit and how to determine how much slippage to include for a market order that occurs as a part of the exit strategy, such as a time exit. We would have to determine what percentage of the trades are stopped out or exited with a market order to determine how much slippage to use.

For example, if we have a strategy that has 50% winners, and takes 1000 trades and exits at one minute before the close each day at the market, we have to determine what percentage of trades actually hit the profit target to determine how much of a slippage factor to use. If 35% of the trades hit the profit target while 15% of the trades exited with a profit one minute before the close (using a market order), while another 40% of trades hit their stop loss and the final 10% of trades exited with a loss one minute before the close and we are using the second back testing option "Fill entire order when trade price exceeds limit price" then we know that 35% of our trades will not get slippage (since those are the ones with a profit target). If we are trading the E-mini S&P, we typically use $25 round turn slippage and commission to account for $20 slippage and $5 commission. We use the $25 factor when cancelling and replacing limit orders to market orders so that we can assume that we will get 1 tick of slippage on the entry minus 1 tick of slippage on the exit. This adds up to $25 just for slippage. We reduce that number to $20 since at least 20% of the trades won't get slippage, based on our experience, especially on stop orders.

The calculation becomes more complex when we factor in the fact that 35% of our trades will not get any slippage if we hold our limit orders until they are filled and use that setting on the back test. The calculation based on this example would show that only 65% of our trades get slippage "for sure". If we consider that 20% of those trades, since some are stop orders will not get slippage, (as we did in the previous paragraph) then we can use an average factor of 80% of 65% = 52%. We multiply that by $25 and add $5 for commission to get $18 round turn slippage and commission or $9 per side on average.

Basically, we are multiplying $25 (for the E-mini S&P or 2 ticks for other markets) times 80% of the trades that would historically get slippage and then adding $5 for commission.

This is an important concept to understand. I know many will want to deduct $50 round turn slippage and commission to be conservative. If you have a trading system that trades frequently, then the average trade profits will be lower. There can be opportunity with strategies that only show $35 average trade profit. If you conservatively assume it has to exceed the $50 threshold, then you can miss out on opportunities to trade

143

higher frequency strategies. (High frequency in the context of 5 - 10 trades per day) Using $50 for slippage and commission is not as much of an issue for a low frequency swing trade strategy that trades 25 times per year with $200 or more average trade profit. The volatility in the equity curve increases on trading systems with higher average trade profits based on longer hold periods and larger stop losses and profit targets.

We use the following settings for back testing and automating the scenario where we hold limit orders until they are filled. There are two different ways to setup automation for this scenario. The first way is in the second image below and the second way is in the third image below. The second way simply holds the limit order until it is filled. In this scenario, if the back testing required price to trade through the limit, then you may received a fill in the real world right at the limit order price but the automated strategy may not show the trading system signal. If it does not show the trading system signal and your limit order gets filled, then the trade will not be managed by the strategy since it does not realize the trade has occurred. The second method shown in the third image below, corrects this as the strategy adopts the real world position and uses the fill price to calculate the strategy exits. With this setup, only one strategy per market can be automated in the same account as it tracks the real world position and multiple positions in the same market would "confuse" the calculation. It is easy enough to create separate accounts to automate different strategies for the same market.

Figure 9-3

Figure 9-4

The following image shows an alternative automation setting and one we recommend if requiring price to trade through the limit order in order to report a fill is the setting that is being used in the Backtesting tab. This automation setting works best since the strategy will not always show a fill if price does not trade through the limit since it is possible to get filled right at the limit (and the strategy is still showing a "flat" position). It is important that the strategy is able to adopt the real world position for the current account so that it can send the appropriate exit orders, otherwise, we are in a position without an automated exit strategy. It is possible to change the back

146

testing setting to "Fill entire order when trade occurs at limit price or better" after the fill takes place.

This would require constant monitoring and it is possible in a fast market or high frequency strategy, the exit order would come before the settings were changed in real time and automation was re-established. One of the disadvantages to using the following option is that only one system per market can be traded in the same account. This is true since it must keep track of the difference between real world position and the strategy position and if multiple systems for the same market are traded in the same account then it would not be possible to know which fill applies to which strategy.

Image created by Tradestation Technologies, the flagship product of Tradestation

Figure 9-5

To reiterate, when automating under the back test approach of "Fill entire order when trade price exceeds limit price Note: When back-testing some fills may occur outside the range of the bar (i.e. above the high or below the low.) This occurs when a limit price is exceeded due to a next bar gap and filling inside of the new bar would introduce an unrealistic price movement)" the strategy will show a fill when back testing a strategy only if the price trades below the limit order for longs or above the limit order for shorts. It is possible that a fill will occur in real trading if the price only trades at your limit order but not through the limit order. The more liquid and larger the order book the more difficult it is to get fills for limit orders. The problem with this scenario is that the trades that would have been filled when trading at the limit order are not accounted for in the back test.

The results when testing using the second option is a close approximation. The results when testing the first option and then cancelling and replacing the limit order to the market once the strategy shows them as filled is more predictable and exact but almost always shows more slippage in a more liquid market such as the E-mini S&P. Less liquid markets can fill limit orders more easily so it can be advantageous to wait for the limit order to be filled before entering trades in less liquid markets. In general, I prefer to cancel and replace limit order entries to the market because I want to be in line with my strategy. This Gap Fill and Reverse strategy originally used a limit order for the E-mini S&P but it has been modified to use a stop order for this reason. As previously stated in this section, I have found in real trading on the E-mini S&P, there is less slippage on stop orders than on cancelling and replacing limit orders to the market.

The setting at the bottom "Stop Orders: Send strategy generated stop orders directly to the Tradestation Order Execution Network" is one additional setting that can be used if you are concerned about having an internet outage and not having a stop loss in the market. This will send the stop order directly to the TradeStation Order Execution Network (instead of being held on your computer within your strategy) and if your internet goes out or if you lose power or if you computer crashes, your stop loss will still be in the market. This will also be the case if you have stop orders that are used for an entry. This can be an issue if the stop order is an entry and your computer goes offline and you enter the market with the stop order on the Tradestation Order Execution Network but have not sent the stop order for the stop loss. You typically do not set and transmit the stop loss stop order until a strategy enters into a trade. In general it is best to have redundancy with backup power and internet or a dedicated server.

We take all of these possibilities into consideration because a market such as the DAX can be very volatile and managing trades in the DAX to reduce slippage can be worth the effort to increase profitability.

We ask ourselves what are the results in the DAX Gap Fill and Reverse if we hold limit orders until the price trades through the limit order. We have the updated performance reports in September 2015 for the DAX Gap Fill and Reverse.

The first Tradestation Performance Summary below shows the results for the DAX Gap Fill and Reverse trading system using the first option when the strategy will "Fill entire order when trade occurs at limit price or better" while the second image below uses the second option "Fill entire order when trade price exceeds limit price". We can see the difference in performance between the two reports.

TradeStation Performance Summary		Expand ▾
All Trades		
Total Net Profit	€24,325.00	Profit Factor	1.49
Gross Profit	€73,825.00	Gross Loss	(€49,500.00)
Total Number of Trades	351	Percent Profitable	52.99%
Winning Trades	186	Losing Trades	165
Even Trades	0		
Avg. Trade Net Profit	€69.30	Ratio Avg. Win:Avg. Loss	1.32
Avg. Winning Trade	€396.91	Avg. Losing Trade	(€300.00)
Largest Winning Trade	€400.00	Largest Losing Trade	(€300.00)
Max. Consecutive Winning Trades	10	Max. Consecutive Losing Trades	9
Avg. Bars in Winning Trades	30.24	Avg. Bars in Losing Trades	0.95
Avg. Bars in Total Trades	20.70		
Max. Shares/Contracts Held	1	Account Size Required	€2,700.00
Return on Initial Capital	24.32%	Annual Rate of Return	2.97%
Return Retracement Ratio	0.19	RINA Index	66130.05
Trading Period	7 Yrs, 3 Mths, 27 Dys, 5 Hrs, 39 Mins	Percent of Time in the Market	0.18%
Max. Equity Run-up	€26,512.50		

Max. Drawdown (Intra-day Peak to Valley)		Max. Drawdown (Trade Close to Trade Close)	
Value	(€3,112.50)	Value	(€2,700.00)
Net Profit as % of Drawdown	781.53%	Net Profit as % of Drawdown	900.93%
Max. Trade Drawdown	(€300.00)		

Equity Curve Line - @FDAX 1 min.(05/07/08 09:31 - 09/04/15 16:00)

Figure 9-6

151

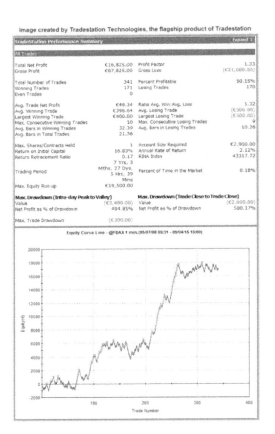

Tradestation Performance Summary			Expand »
All Trades			
Total Net Profit	€16,825.00	Profit Factor	1.33
Gross Profit	€67,825.00	Gross Loss	(€51,000.00)
Total Number of Trades	341	Percent Profitable	50.15%
Winning Trades	171	Losing Trades	170
Even Trades	0		
Avg. Trade Net Profit	€49.34	Ratio Avg. Win:Avg. Loss	1.32
Avg. Winning Trade	€396.64	Avg. Losing Trade	(€300.00)
Largest Winning Trade	€400.00	Largest Losing Trade	(€300.00)
Max. Consecutive Winning Trades	10	Max. Consecutive Losing Trades	9
Avg. Bars in Winning Trades	32.39	Avg. Bars in Losing Trades	10.26
Avg. Bars in Total Trades	21.36		
Max. Shares/Contracts Held	1	Account Size Required	€2,900.00
Return on Initial Capital	16.83%	Annual Rate of Return	2.12%
Return Retracement Ratio	0.17	RINA Index	43317.72
Trading Period	7 Yrs, 3 Mths, 27 Dys, 5 Hrs, 39 Mins	Percent of Time in the Market	0.18%
Max. Equity Run-up	€19,500.00		
Max. Drawdown (Intra-day Peak to Valley)		**Max. Drawdown (Trade Close to Trade Close)**	
Value	(€3,400.00)	Value	(€2,900.00)
Net Profit as % of Drawdown	494.85%	Net Profit as % of Drawdown	580.17%
Max. Trade Drawdown	(€300.00)		

Figure 9-7

The two reports in this section do not include slippage and commission. We do this to accurately determine the difference in average trade net profit between the reports to determine which one is better. We see that in the first report, the average trade profit is 69.30 Euros while in the second report, the average trade profit is 49.34 Euros. There is about a 20 Euro difference in average trade profit between the two reports, with

the first report showing fills for all limits if the price touches the limit order while the second report is requiring price to trade through the limit order. The difference in slippage for the DAX could easily be 1 tick on entry and 1 tick on exit or 25 Euros. The conclusion could be that the second scenario is a more profitable way to trade since it does not include all the trades that are potentially filled in live trading at the limit and price never trades through. There are 10 less trades in the second report. This means that there are about 10 trades that traded at the limit but not through the limit order.
Some of those may have been filled in the real world.

The conclusion may be to have a separate account just for this strategy since there could be more than 1 tick of slippage in a volatile market like the DAX and holding limit orders until they are filled instead of cancelling and replacing the limit orders to the market in a strategy like this where we are trading a volatile market and there are only a few ticks of average trade profit.

If we add 30 Euros of slippage and commission to the first scenario where we report fills at the limit price (and not through the limit) and then in automation, cancel and replace limits to the market, and include 12.5 Euros or 1 tick of slippage on entry and 12.5 Euros or 1 tick of slippage on exit and 5 Euros for commission then our average trade profit becomes 39.30 Euros. I realize the DAX is volatile and "wobbly" and there are many cases of more slippage but there are many cases of even fills and even negative slippage (that goes in our favor and we get a better fill price) in this type of market so it can average out to 30 Euros.

If we add 11.25 Euros of slippage and commission to the second scenario where we report fills only if they trade through the limit price and in automation we hold them until filled, then 0 Euros of slippage and commission would be included on entry and 6.25 Euros or 1/2 tick of slippage would be included on exit and 5 Euros included for commission. This would bring our average trade profit to 38.11 Euros. You may ask, "how can you average a ½ a tick of slippage". We consider that half of the trades hit its profit target where the limit order is held until it trades through the limit order price and half of the trades are stopped out or use a time exit. Half of the time we get 12.50 slippage and half of the time we get no slippage on the exit. This is why we use an average of 6.25.

If we just look at the average trade profits based on these calculations, we would conclude that the first scenario is better by 1.19 Euros. The results would essentially be the same. We have to consider the fact that there are potentially "free trades" in the second scenario. We use the term "free trade" to describe a trade where a limit order is filled at the trade price in real world trading that does not show up in the back test when requiring the price to trade through the limit in order to report a fill. With the additional free trades and the potential for increased slippage beyond our 1 tick of estimated slippage, the conclusion could be made to trade using the second scenario setup. Since the results are still relatively close based on average trade profit, the first scenario could also be used since setting up a different account for each strategy may be cumbersome and increase the potential for errors if you are less experienced in automating multiple strategies.

Another example of a higher frequency strategy that makes this concept even clearer and shows how important it is to make sure that the average trade profit is high enough, is based on one of our proprietary strategies, New York Scalper.

In the first image, we see the Tradestation Performance Report trading this strategy with historical limit order testing using the first option "Fill entire order when trade occurs at limit price or better". The second image shows the results of the strategy "Fill entire order when trade price exceeds limit price".

In a strategy like this, real results can be somewhere between the two reports. If we look at this from the perspective of an average trade profit and take the average of the two reports, there would be $2 average trade profit. This is before commission and slippage for stop orders. In the end, it would not be a profitable strategy. The average trade profit in the first report is only $10.68 with no slippage or commission. We need to see at least $35 average trade profit for a strategy in the E-mini S&P to have any interest in the strategy.

Figure 9-8

156

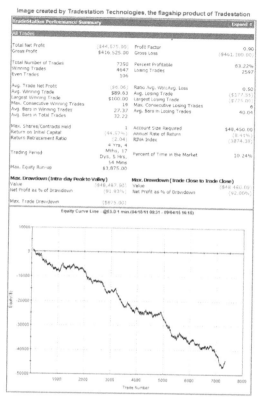

Figure 9-9

Setting it up in NinjaTrader

When NinjaTrader back tests a trading strategy, by default it reports a fill for a limit order only when the historical price trades through the limit order price. This is known as the Default Fill Type and can be selected as the first option in the drop down menu under Historical Fill Processing and Fill Type that can be found when setting up the strategy inputs. This is

157

different than the way Tradestation back tests limit orders by default and is considered a more conservative approach. When developing, testing, and automating trading systems in different platforms, it is important to understand the differences between the platforms and how strategies can be tested. Additional differences can be related to the code differences in the platform and the data differences between data feeds that are used for the historical data. Live data differences can also provide slightly different results at times.

The default fill type that is used in NinjaTrader is the same way Tradestation back tests when using the second option shown in Figure 9-3 on page 118. Strategies can be tested this way as a more conservative scenario.

Another way we can test strategies in NinjaTrader is to test them similar to Tradestation's default method shown in Figure 9-1 on page 114. In order to do this, we have created our own Custom Fill Type called, LiberalWithOpen fill type. This is a more liberal method for testing and shows a fill when the trade price occurs at the limit order without trading through the limit order. In order to automate this sort of testing, we must also setup a method for cancelling and replacing orders in NinjaTrader for limit orders that are not filled after a given number of seconds. NinjaTrader allows us to customize and develop different fill types. The NinjaScript below is a screen shot of the LiberalWithOpen fill type.

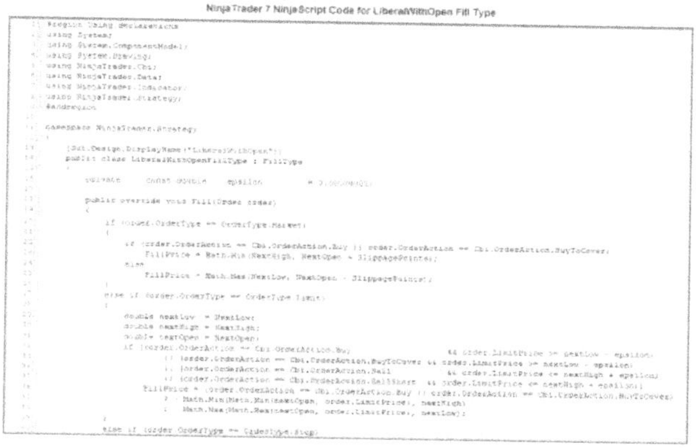

Figure 9-10

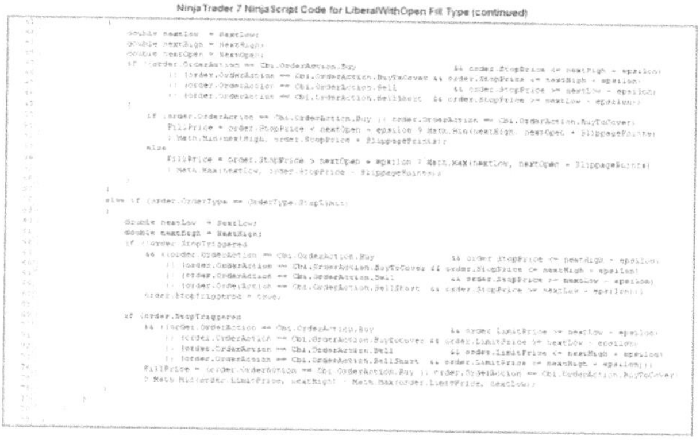

Figure 9-11

It is not necessary to understand the code above to use it. The code can be downloaded from the website http://algorithmictradingsystemscom.com. More details on downloading the code from the website are in Chapter 16.

159

Once the code has been created it can be placed in the following directory.

NinjaTrader 7/bin/Custom/Type

Next, re-start NinjaTrader so that NinjaTrader can "see" the new fill type. To use the LiberalWithOpen fill type, it can be selected in the strategy drop down list. From the image below, you can see the fill types are Default, Liberal, and Liberal With Open. We use two of these fill types that we have discussed in this chapter: Default or LiberalWithOpen.

Figure 9-12

Next we take a look at the performance summary and equity curves for NY Scalper trading system in NinjaTrader and compare the results based on the fill types of Default and LiberalWithOpen. We see similar results for this trading system that we saw in Tradestation using different fill types in order to test for limit order entries.

First we show the performance for this strategy using the LiberalWithOpen fill type followed by the performance for the Default fill type. The code for this strategy is not included since it is proprietary and NY Scalper is a case study for the principle of testing limit order fills.

NY Scalper Trading System Performance Summary with Liberal Fill Type in NinjaTrader 7

Currency | Summary | Graphs | Executions | Trades | Periods | Orders

Performance	All Trades	Long Trades	Short Trades
Total Net Profit	$141576.55	$76213.42	$65463.14
Gross Profit	$658883.83	$340262.18	$318600.46
Gross Loss	$-517181.58	$-264048.77	[illegible]
Commission	$0.00	$0.00	$0.00
Profit Factor	1.27	1.29	1.26
Cumulative Profit	$141576.55	$76213.41	$65463.13
Max. Drawdown	[illegible]	[illegible]	[illegible]
Sharpe Ratio	1.26	0.94	1.04
Start Date	4/18/2011		
End Date	9/4/2015		
Total # of Trades	12042	6040	6002
Percent Profitable	69.04%	70.75%	67.32%
# of Winning Trades	8312	4273	4039
# of Losing Trades	3728	1767	1961
Average Trade	$11.77	$12.62	$10.91
Average Winning Trade	$79.27	$79.63	$78.88
Average Losing Trade	$-139.73	$-141.47	$-125.20
Ratio avg. Win / avg. Loss	0.57	0.56	0.61
Max. conseq. Winners	24	24	17
Max. conseq. Losers	9	7	6
Largest Winning Trade	$1237.50	$1237.50	$1012.50
Largest Losing Trade	[illegible]	[illegible]	[illegible]
# of Trades per Day	7.52	3.77	3.75
Avg. Time in Market	30.7 min	29.9 min	31.5 min
Avg. Bars in Trade	30.7	29.9	31.5
Profit per Month	$2638.02	$1461.57	$1247.11
Max. Time to Recover	65.07 days	59.58 days	58.13 days
Average MAE	[illegible]	[illegible]	[illegible]
Average MFE	$81.48	$81.99	$80.98
Average ETD	[illegible]	[illegible]	[illegible]

Figure 9-13

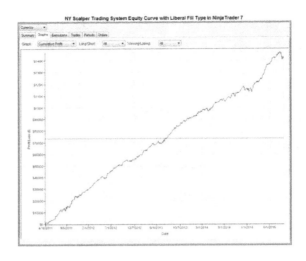

NY Scalper Trading System Equity Curve with Liberal Fill Type in NinjaTrader 7

Figure 9-14

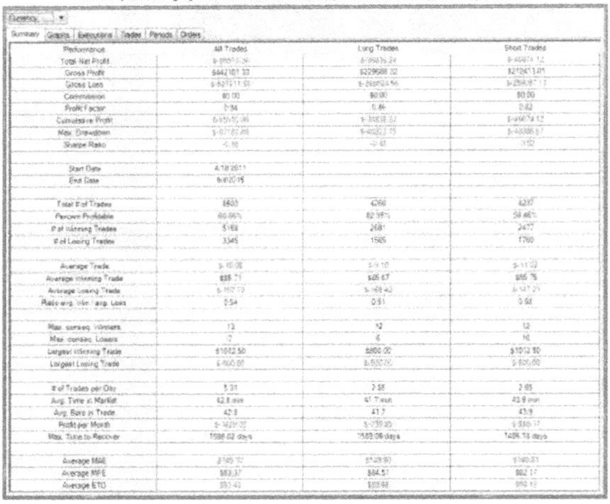

NY Scalper Trading System Performance Summary with Default Fill Type in NinjaTrader 7

Figure 9-15

162

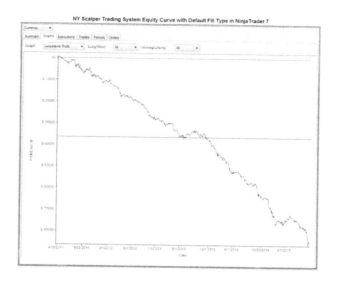

Figure 9-16

For this strategy, we come to the same conclusion that we did with the Tradestation version. The actual results will end up somewhere between the two results. Without any additional slippage and commission, this may be around breakeven. Once you add slippage and commission, then the results will be negative.

A more complex approach could include using stop orders on tick charts so that once the price traded to your limit price, a stop order could be placed one tick in the direction of the trade that will be taken. For example, for long trades, if your limit order is to go long at 2101.00 in the E-mini S&P, wait until it trades down to 2099.75 and then place a stop order one tick

163

higher. The market could trade down on a tick by tick basis before it trades up a single tick to hit your stop and you could get filled at a lower price. Another scenario is that it could trade down to 2101.00 and then move higher so that your trade is never filled if you required it to trade down to 2099.75. To make sure that you didn't miss the trade, you could start placing a stop order one tick higher than the current price once it hit 2100 instead of 2099.75. Testing strategies on one tick charts can be memory intensive. I recommend doing this only to fine tune a strategy or for higher frequency strategies. For short trades, we would do the opposite. If we wanted to short the E-mini S&P at 2100.00, the conservative approach would wait for it to trade up to 2101.25 and then place a sell stop 1 tick below that closing price on one tick charts. A more aggressive approach, so that the trade isn't missed, is to place a stop order one tick below the current price once the price hits 2100.00 at 2099.75. In each case you could place a limit order instead of a stop order so that you are placing a limit order 1 tick above the market for longs and 1 tick below the market for shorts so that essentially you are place a limit order at the offer for longs and a limit order at the bid for shorts, so that you don't give up anymore slippage. If you place a limit order, you will get filled right away. If you place a stop order, you will at times get better fills. For example, if you are placing a long trade one tick above the current price once the market hits 2100.00, the market could go down 3 ticks (just as an example) to 2099.75...2099.50...2099.25 before there is an uptick, which would give you a fill at 2099.50.

If we automate a trading system in NinjaTrader using the results from the LiberalWithOpen fill type, we must code the strategy so that it will cancel and replace the limit orders to market orders if they are not filled within a given number of seconds, usually between 0 – 3 seconds. We compare this setup with the setup we use in Tradestation in Figure 9-2 on page 115. In NinjaTrader we can customize order handling.

In this chapter, we don't show the code but the settings that we use to do this. The code for cancelling and replacing limit orders to the market can be found in the Gap Fill and Reverse strategies in the previous chapters. Many times we refer to the Gap Fill and Reverse strategy as Gap Fill Fade to shorten the name. It can also be abbreviated as GapFR or GapFF. We see in the image below that inputs 23 and 25 should be set to True and inputs 24 and 26 can be set to a number between 0 and 3 seconds or potentially longer such as 15 seconds. The longer that you wait, the further away the price can move and a winning trade could be missed. It depends on the market and the depth of the order book as well as the spread between the bid and offer. Most of the strategies that we automate have a bid and offer at every price and we use 0 to 3 seconds.

Figure 9-17

10. How Profit Targets Affect Trading Performance

Let's face it, it "feels" really good to grab a winning trade quickly. Many traders believe that using **"tight"** profit targets are a profitable way to trade. It can be a profitable way to trade,

166

if it is based on a tested strategy, but many times (not for every market or every situation) it is inferior to holding the trade for a longer period of time. It is easy to look at a short period of time and see how a trade should have been exited with a profit and how "frustrating" it was to see a "nice" gain turn into a losing trade. After experiencing this scenario a few times, it is easy to come to the conclusion that it is better to have a profit target, tighter stop loss, trailing stop loss, and/or a breakeven stop loss. Market analysis should not be based on short term windows of a few trades or how it makes you feel.

Speaking of feelings, trading psychology is important and there are two solutions to this scenario. **The first is to let your system run** without watching the results tick by tick. Watching the market fluctuations and feeling good when you see the profits and feeling bad during losing streaks or drawdowns will make it difficult to follow a trading system for a long period of time as this inevitable roller coaster will become too frustrating to tolerate and proliferate a manic depressant attitude.

The second solution to this problem is to use a profit target, even if the results are inferior to not using a profit target. If using a profit target more closely matches your trading psychology and ability to stick with the trading system, then using a planned profit target that works will yield better results than trading without a plan or making emotional "overrides" to your trading system. There are time periods in the market where there are very few trends and the price action can become very choppy. During these market conditions, a strategy with profit targets will usually outperform a strategy without a profit target since prices continually return to the prices from which they came.

In previous chapters we developed the Gap Fill and Reverse with Limit Orders trading system on Crude Oil. What does the performance look like if we add a $500 profit target? We can simply set the profit target to True and use a $500 profit target. We can also write code to trade multiple contracts and exit half at the profit target and half at the end of the day. We will do this as well in a later chapter.

First we will take a look at the Gap Fill and Reverse trading system with profit targets on a single contract since it is important to look at each scenario with profit targets separately so that we can see the isolated effect of adding a profit target.

To quantify and fully understand what I am saying about the effects of profit targets we will demonstrate the results of the Gap Fill and Reverse Crude Oil with Limit Orders trading system with different profit targets in order to make this principle more clear. In the next few pages, there are Tradestation Performance Summaries using different profit target levels. The first performance summary is the strategy without profit targets for our frame of reference followed by the same strategy with profit targets from $100 - $500 in $100 increments and then a $1000 profit target based performance summary. Screen shots of the Performance Summary and the Performance Graph from the Tradestation Performance Reports are also included since the equity curve can provide good information about the quality of a trading system. **The original analysis for this strategy testing and chapter was done in 2013 which is reflected in the reports.**

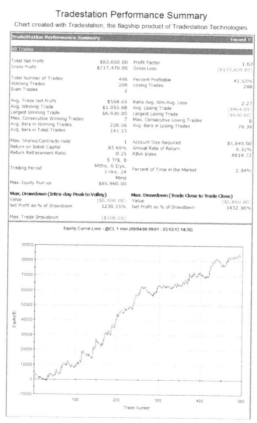

Figure 10-1

Tradestation Performance Summary

Chart created with Tradestation, the flagship product of Tradestation Technologies

Figure 10-2

170

Tradestation Performance Summary

Chart created with Tradestation, the flagship product of Tradestation Technologies

Figure 10-3

171

Tradestation Performance Summary

Chart created with Tradestation, the flagship product of Tradestation Technologies

Figure 10-4

172

Tradestation Performance Summary

Chart created with Tradestation, the flagship product of Tradestation Technologies

Figure 10-5

173

Tradestation Performance Summary

Chart Created on Tradestation, the flagship product of Tradestation Technologies

Tradestation Performance Summary		Expand
All Trades		
Total Net Profit	$30,780.00	Profit Factor	1.29
Gross Profit	$135,440.00	Gross Loss	($104,080.00)
Total Number of Trades	497	Percent Profitable	56.34%
Winning Trades	280	Losing Trades	217
Even Trades	0		
Avg. Trade Net Profit	$61.89	Ratio Avg. Win:Avg. Loss	1.00
Avg. Winning Trade	$483.71	Avg. Losing Trade	($482.40)
Largest Winning Trade	$870.00	Largest Losing Trade	($500.00)
Max. Consecutive Winning Trades	12	Max. Consecutive Losing Trades	8
Avg. Bars in Winning Trades	62.96	Avg. Bars in Losing Trades	56.51
Avg. Bars in Total Trades	60.14		
Max. Shares/Contracts Held	1	Account Size Required	$5,140.00
Return on Initial Capital	30.76%	Annual Rate of Return	4.11%
Return Retracement Ratio	0.21	RINA Index	10769.52
Trading Period	6 Yrs, 6 Mths, 7 Dys, 3 Hrs, 13 Mins	Percent of Time in the Market	0.86%
Max. Equity Run-up	$33,130.00		

Max. Drawdown (Intra-day Peak to Valley)		**Max. Drawdown (Trade Close to Trade Close)**	
Value	($5,860.00)	Value	($5,140.00)
Net Profit as % of Drawdown	524.91%	Net Profit as % of Drawdown	598.44%
Max. Trade Drawdown	($500.00)		

Equity Curve Line : @CL 1 min.(09/04/06 09:01 - 03/15/13 14:30)

$500 Profit Target

Figure 10-7

It is clear that the results most traders would prefer are in the original strategy, without a profit target. Some of the patterns in the performance results are clear as **we highlight three of these performance summary relationships below**.

1.) The smaller the profit target the higher the accuracy of the trading system. The $100 profit target shows 85% accuracy while our original strategy shows only 41% accuracy. As we incrementally increase the profit target, the % accuracy incrementally decreases.

Profit Target	% Profitable
$ 100.00	85.69%
$ 200.00	73.99%
$ 300.00	66.33%
$ 400.00	60.16%
$ 500.00	56.34%
$ 1,000.00	45.07%
No Profit Target	41.53%

Figure 10-8

2.) The smaller the profit target the lower the average trade profit. As we decrease the maximum profit allowed with a tighter and tighter profit target, we lower the average trade profit for profitable trades which then lowers the average trade profit for all trades.

Profit Target	Avg Trade Profit
$ 100.00	$14.15
$ 200.00	$19.31
$ 300.00	$32.74
$ 400.00	$45.81
$ 500.00	$61.89
$ 1,000.00	$97.59
No Profit Target	$168.65

Figure 10-9

3.) The smaller the profit target the lower the Net Profit as a % of Drawdown. This is the Total Net Profit divided by Drawdown

176

and one of the main factors that we look for in a trading systems success. Smaller profit targets prevent us from capturing the larger winners and affect the ability of the trading system to maximize profits.

Profit Target	Net Profit/DrawD
$ 100.00	203.48%
$ 200.00	234.23%
$ 300.00	282.93%
$ 400.00	375.12%
$ 500.00	524.91%
$ 1,000.00	766.19%
No Profit Target	1230.15%

Figure 10-10

The overall advantage goes to our original strategy without a profit target. This means that trading a system that is "right" less than 50% of the time can be more profitable than trading a system that is right 85% of the time.

This is the case for many trading systems. The desire to be right can frequently "penalize" you as a trader. Managing the trade by cutting losses quickly and giving your position as much room to maximize the profits is what consistently shows the best results in most of our trading systems research. Looking at 1000's of performance summaries and scenarios similar to the ones we have looked at in this chapter usually show the same type of results - larger or no profit targets (for day trade systems that exit at the end of the day) have better results related to two of

177

the most important trading performance statistics: Average Trade Profit and Net profit as % of Drawdown.

There are exceptions to every rule, especially in the stock indexes, notably the E-mini S&P futures, and markets that become very choppy or have narrow ranges. This Gap Fill and Reverse strategy is one of those exceptions that works well with a $200 profit target on the E-mini S&P. What happens if we take out the profit target in the Gap Fill and Reverse Using Limit Orders for the E-mini S&P? The results are shown below.

Tradestation Performance Summary

Chart created with Tradestation, the flagship product of Tradestation Technologies

Figure 10-11

We see that average trade profit actually drops from $58.41 down to $40.14 and we lose over 1000% on the Net Profit divided by the Drawdown since the drawdown increases from less than $2,000 to slightly greater than $5,000. The percentage accuracy also drops. The strategy does not work as well for the first 200 trades when the profit target is removed.

179

Additional Risks

One of the things you may or may not have noticed in the reports for Crude Oil for the strategies using profit targets of $400 and $500 is that the largest winning trade is $870. How can this be since we have a profit target of $400 and $500 or exit by the end of the day? The largest trade on the performance summary with a $400 profit target should be $400 and the largest winning trade on the performance summary with a $500 profit target should be $500. It is important to take a look at the largest winning trade and largest losing trade to see if they match the profit target and stop loss. These two numbers can also tell you if slippage and commission have been included. For example a strategy with a $500 profit target and $500 stop loss would show the largest winning trade as $475 and largest losing trade as $525 if a $25 round turn slippage and commission factor was used in a single contract trading system. The performance summaries in this chapter have not used any slippage and commission factors.

The way we can find out why there is a largest winning trade of $870 instead of $400 or $500 is to take a look at the Maximum Adverse Excursion Trade Graph from the Tradestation Performance Summary.

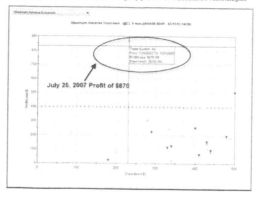

Maximum Adverse Excursion for Gap Fill and Reverse Crude Oil $400 profit

Chart created with Tradestation, the flagship product of Tradestation Technologies

July 25, 2007 Profit of $870

Figure 10-12

We see that on July 25, 2007 that there was a profit of $870. We go to the chart and take a look at that particular trade. We see below that on July 25, 2007, there was an intra-day gap in Crude Oil. On this particular day, there was an exchange outage for electronic trading on NYMEX. When the market re-opened, the price was above the profit target of $400 and $500 so those trades exited with an $870 profit. The profit targets of $300 and below exited their trades at the profit target before the exchange outage.

181

Figure 10-13

The reason we take time to point this out is to understand how to troubleshoot strategies by looking at Trade Graphs such as Maximum Adverse Excursion and to understand the additional risk in trading. Exchange outages do not happen frequently and in this case the result was positive for our strategy and the profit was larger than we had planned on with our profit target. There can be times when an exchange outage, internet outage, power outage, or a computer crash could increase your trading risk. The market could go in the opposite direction of your trade and the opportunity to exit the trade could take place at prices that extend beyond your stop loss point and increasing your risk by the time your computer or the exchange comes back online. If the market is beyond your profit target exit point then it

182

increases your profit. If it is below your stop loss then it increases your loss for that trade.

I find that over time, situations like these tend to balance out historically with half of the errors going against me while the other half of the errors going in my favor and the total profit and loss for errors is around breakeven over time. Any given year can see a big deviation and the errors could all be in my favor or they could all be against me for an extended period of time. Exchange outages have are very rare but are still a risk parameter in trading. The more controllable risk factors that we mentioned: such as internet outages, power outages, or computer crashes can be reduced and managed with redundant computers, redundant internet connections, and battery backups for power supplies. These redundancies can reduce our risk. A dedicated server is another option that can provide even greater redundancy and minimize down time.

Exchange outages for the electronic markets which have become extremely rare could be hedged by taking the opposite position in the pit markets or by trading similar instruments on different exchanges. For example, during the September 11, 2001 terrorist attacks on the twin towers in New York City, all of the US Exchanges closed for several days. The European markets stayed open. A long position in the US stock index futures could have been hedged by trading a European stock index such as the DAX by shorting the DAX with an equivalent notional value of your long position in US stock index futures. For Crude Oil, if the NYMEX goes out, it is possible to trade Brent on the ICE Europe exchange by taking the opposite position.

As I update this chapter in 2015, many of the pit markets are going away so trading similar contracts in foreign futures is still one way to "hedge" or take an offsetting position in a similar market.

.

11.   Big Profit Targets

In the previous chapter we looked at how profit targets can limit profits but noticed that as we expanded the profit target to much larger values, the strategy performance started to match the performance of the system without profit targets. For example: when you compare the results of the Gap Fill and Reverse Crude Oil without the profit target versus using a $1000 profit target, the emphasis was on the fact that "tight" or "small" profit targets reduced the average trade to the point of being unprofitable after slippage and commission.

Relative terminology such as "tight" or "small" should be defined. **The smallest profit target that we have used in any market condition is $200 per futures contract.** We mainly use profit targets this small on stock index based systems or on strategies where we trade multiple contracts and use $200 per contract as the first profit target since there are times when a market can become very trendless or choppy for a year or more and the profit target version will help our equity curve.

Large profit targets can also improve trading systems. My mindset has been biased over the years to keep a system simple and "raw" and not use many parameters or exit strategies,

185

letting the strategy run until the end of a trading period and with a stop loss. When I first began trading, it was during a period of expanding daily ranges. My strategy testing showed that using any profit targets on any of my systems reduced the performance of the strategy. After experiencing a drastic drop in daily ranges and a drop in volatility, I have learned over the years that adding profit targets can be beneficial to trading systems, even when the historical results are better without the profit target.

One of the biggest keys to trading systems is the ability to handle changes in volatility. Managing changes in volatility can be more difficult and is more critical than the actual change in trend. The patterns in the market can change when ranges are very narrow versus very wide. Trading the S&P when the daily ranges are 30 points is much different than trading when the daily ranges are only 10 points or less. When ranges are narrow and decreasing, entering trades using counter trend entry methods and exiting with profit targets has been beneficial. When the daily ranges are expanding, entering trades using trend, momentum, and countertrend entry methods with larger profit targets or end of day exits has shown the best results.

One of the popular pearls of wisdom on Wall Street among traders is **"do not let a profit turn into a loss".** I would modify this by saying **"do not let a significant profit turn into a loss".**

Are you going to move your stop to breakeven after just 1 tick of profit? If we don't move our stop to breakeven after 1 tick, should it be 2 ticks? Tight breakeven stop losses can also drastically reduce the quality of a trading system. "Letting go" to the point of not getting "tangled" up in volatility is necessary to let the system breathe. Moving a stop to breakeven should be done after a "significant profit" has occurred.

"Significant profit" now needs to be defined. This is not a number that is meaningful to you and what you feel like you need in your personal life in order to buy something on your wish list or to buy something you need. This is a number that is based on price action and the character of the market that you are trading. The market does not care about you and what you want and cannot be "engineered" or imposed upon by your demands or wishes. For every $100 per day that you make in any endeavor yields about $25,000 per year since there are about 250 business days per year. Many new traders begin to do the math and say, "Just $100 per contract per day times 4 contracts is $100,000 per year and that will replace my day job". That is only 2 points on the E-mini S&P! It sounds so easy! What is wrong with this sort of math? You will not be able to make money every day. If you set a $100 daily profit target per contract, what happens when the market goes against you and your trade never shows even 1 tick of profit? Where is your stop loss? Now you have to double up the next day to make up for it. Then you have two losing days in a row so you have to make

187

four times as much the following day to keep the pace. Now you are starting to risk more than you anticipated and your emotions become a factor.

The point is that the market will not give you want you want. Trading is about taking what the market gives and trading around the current conditions of the market. I hear many traders say, I just want to make 10% per month or an extra $2,000 or $3,000 per month. I have not found it possible to normalize returns and plan on specific dollar or percentage returns. We have losing weeks and months. Also 10% per month is 120% per year and while it is possible to do this, expecting to repeat this year in and year out is not realistic.

Also, as an exception to what I am saying is that there may be traders who, for a period of time, are able to make a specific percentage return each month. One method that can make this possible is option writing. It is true that option writers can go on a long winning streak of steady returns of 2% - 10% or more per month for an extend period of several years. For most traders who use this method, a volatility event can provide a huge setback in returns as well as a drawdown, and such an event can create losses that give back several years of profits.

I have also seen some of the best traders go on some long winning streaks where they did make money every day with astronomical returns on small accounts for an extended period of time. There are traders who win trading contests and seem to defy the odds. There are certain market conditions that can provide many traders with rags to riches stories. The late 90's and the dot com bubble is evidence of this in the equity markets.

As traders, we have to be flexible in our trading and learn the characteristics of the market so that we can take what it offers while simultaneously being comfortable with the risk we need to take in order to have a chance to benefit from our trading systems. Previously I stated that most day trading systems that I have use at least a $300 stop loss per contract. Some use higher stop losses of $800 or more per contract. When trading a system with an $800 stop loss, do we exit when it is down $500? You may test your system and realize it isn't very profitable with a $500 stop loss but it is profitable with an $800 stop loss. You may then decide to enter the system only when it is down $500 but soon learn that using that approach may not work out as well either since there are a significant number of trades that begin to be profitable right from the entry price that will be missed when waiting for an intratrade drawdown.

I have started this chapter with an explanation of trading system expectations to emphasize what I have found to be true in the markets in my testing. The next example is a strategy called SR CounterTrend Crude Oil. We use this countertrend strategy to trade Crude Oil and have discovered after giving some large profits back that a big profit target works best in this trading system. SR means Support and Resistance so this strategy will enter long trades near our support levels and enter short trades near our resistance levels. This is one of our favorite day trading systems and uses a $500 stop loss, a $500 breakeven stop loss or exits at 3:10 pm EST. We can enter up to two trades per day on this system.

As you know the Crude Oil market can be very volatile and can have the tendency to "rip your head off". It is important to carefully manage your trades as well as your risk in this fast paced market. Many times this system will go back to our breakeven stop loss and then re-enter, meaning we can frequently give back $500+ in profits. This is necessary in order to give the system enough room to capture the larger winners. Over time we noticed that it can give back some even larger winners of nearly $1500 or more. When I re-tested this trading system, I realized that using a "big" profit made this strategy more profitable. One of the keys to using this big profit target was that the strategy could re-enter trades so if we exited with a large profit target then we have the chance to re-enter a second trade on another pull back. Below is a screen shot of trading on April 18, 2013 showing how our first trade showed nearly $1500 in profit per contract, then reversed to the breakeven point, re-entered for a second trade which was stopped out for a $500 loss. The trading for this strategy on April 18, 2013 can be seen below.

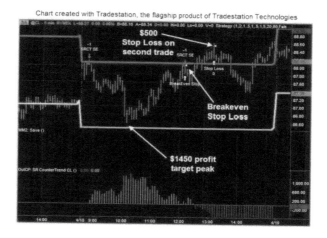

Figure 11-1

Next we take a look at the Tradestation Performance Summary for this trading system and see that even though this strategy gives back some good trades, the historical performance since 9/5/2006 (the beginning of electronic trading during the day on Crude Oil futures) shows good results. We show the performances for both the original strategy without a profit target and the strategy with an $800 profit target so that the results can be compared.

191

Tradestation Performance Summary

Chart created on Tradestation, the flagship product of Tradestation Technologies

TradeStation Performance Summary		Expand ▼
All Trades		
Total Net Profit	$67,345.00	Profit Factor	1.56
Gross Profit	$187,265.00	Gross Loss	($119,920.00)
Total Number of Trades	623	Percent Profitable	37.72%
Winning Trades	235	Losing Trades	388
Even Trades	0		
Avg. Trade Net Profit	$108.10	Ratio Avg. Win:Avg. Loss	2.58
Avg. Winning Trade	$796.87	Avg. Losing Trade	($309.07)
Largest Winning Trade	$4,895.00	Largest Losing Trade	($975.00)
Max. Consecutive Winning Trades	5	Max. Consecutive Losing Trades	18
Avg. Bars in Winning Trades	31.31	Avg. Bars in Losing Trades	14.27
Avg. Bars in Total Trades	20.70		
Max. Shares/Contracts Held	1	Account Size Required	$5,450.00
Return on Initial Capital	67.35%	Annual Rate of Return	7.78%
Return Retracement Ratio	0.25	RINA Index	10838.45
Trading Period	6 Yrs, 7 Mths, 12 Dys, 2 Hrs, 30 Mins	Percent of Time in the Market	1.77%
Max. Equity Run-up	$69,920.00		

Max. Drawdown (Intra-day Peak to Valley)		**Max. Drawdown (Trade Close to Trade Close)**	
Value	($6,115.00)	Value	($5,450.00)
Net Profit as % of Drawdown	1101.31%	Net Profit as % of Drawdown	1235.69%
Max. Trade Drawdown	($500.00)		

Equity Curve Line - @CL 5 min.(09/05/06 08:36 - 04/19/13 15:15)

No Profit Target

Figure 11-2

Tradestation Performance Summary

Chart created on Tradestation, the flagship product of Tradestation Technologies

Figure 11-3

We can see that when adding the profit target the drawdown is decreased by about $1600 while the total net profit and average trade profit is also decreased but the Net Profit as % of Drawdown is increased. The percentage of profitable trades also goes up when we add the profit target. This is a case that shows how a large profit target is slightly better than no profit target.

Below is an optimization report of profit targets from $200 to $2000 in $100 increments. We do this to show the results of using profit targets at different levels. In the previous performance summary we showed the results of a profit target of $800. This is only the 4th best performance summary result based on the far right column and average trade profit. If we use $1200, we improve the system beyond the original strategy.

	NO. SR CounterTrend Crude PrfTgAmt	All Net Profit	All Total Trades	All % Profitable	All Win/Loss Ratio	All Avg Trade	All Max Intraday Drawdown	All ProfitFactor	All Return on Account
1	1,200	71,440.00	628	41.40	2.27	113.76	-4,592.50	1.60	1,556.97
2	700	62,210.00	634	51.10	1.46	98.12	-3,997.50	1.52	1,556.22
3	600	58,730.00	638	55.64	1.19	92.05	-3,947.50	1.50	1,487.78
4	800	61,520.00	630	46.83	1.73	97.65	-4,302.50	1.52	1,429.87
5	1,100	63,950.00	628	41.56	2.17	101.83	-4,582.50	1.54	1,395.53
6	1,000	63,660.00	628	42.83	2.05	101.37	-4,582.50	1.54	1,389.20
7	900	63,220.00	628	44.43	1.92	100.67	-4,582.50	1.54	1,379.60
8	500	52,756.00	641	62.25	0.88	82.35	-3,942.50	1.44	1,338.87
9	1,300	69,520.00	628	40.61	2.32	110.70	-5,592.50	1.58	1,243.09
10	2,000	68,060.00	624	38.14	2.55	109.07	-5,592.50	1.57	1,218.99
11	1,900	67,010.00	624	38.14	2.54	107.39	-5,592.50	1.56	1,198.21
12	1,400	65,495.00	627	39.71	2.35	104.46	-5,592.50	1.55	1,171.12
13	1,800	64,310.00	624	38.14	2.50	103.06	-5,592.50	1.54	1,149.93
14	1,600	63,145.00	625	38.72	2.42	101.03	-5,592.50	1.53	1,129.10
15	1,500	63,140.00	626	39.14	2.38	100.86	-5,592.50	1.53	1,129.01
16	1,700	60,620.00	624	38.14	2.46	97.15	-5,592.50	1.51	1,083.95
17	400	42,120.00	648	66.05	0.71	65.00	-4,562.50	1.39	923.18
18	300	28,650.00	660	70.81	0.54	43.41	-5,767.50	1.30	496.75
19	200	14,525.00	675	77.33	0.35	21.52	-6,462.50	1.19	224.76

Figure 11-4

There is something to be said about large profit targets. We rarely see profits greater than $1200 and that is a significant level in which we do not want to give back profits for a day trade system. This could be said about any profit target for $600 or more since at $600 the average trade profit with slippage and commission is still greater than $90 and the return on account

194

(based on drawdown size) is still large as we see from the optimization report above.

We also see that the largest losing trade in both reports is $525, even though we are using a $500 stop loss. This indicates that $25 round turn slippage and commission is factored into the report and with a profit target; the average trade profit is almost $100 per trade per contract. In real trading we find that using $25 round turn slippage and commission is sufficient as there is a large standard deviation of slippage factors in Crude Oil and while some trades get slippage of $50 or more per contract, sometimes we get negative slippage (or slippage in our favor) of $40 or more per contract. This is to say that even though Crude Oil is a fast and volatile market, we have found that strategies with these numbers work well in real trading.

SR CounterTrend is one of our proprietary trading systems and we use this as an example of a real world trading system that we have used for a while and how profit targets affect a trading system.

12.   Going Broke Taking Profits

There is a popular saying on Wall Street that says **"You Can't Go Broke Taking Profits"**. This may be true for a long term investor who invests long only in the stock market and gets out near market highs and months later is able to "re-invest" at better and lower prices. Market timing is tough even for long term investors and this scenario might sound great but it is difficult to implement. The one time that your market position is exited near cyclical or even all time highs, in anticipation of a pullback, could be the one time before the next bull market surge where there is a price separation from "old" prices and a place where the market never returns. In the process of trading in and out of the market for example, 10 long trades for a 3% gain each time or a 30% total return (this is only an example), the market may now surge 30%, 40%, 50%+ up to new levels and never provide the "pullback" for re-investment. The overall return in this example would have been lower than a buy and hold approach. There is an argument to be made for holding part of your portfolio in a long term position in the stock market.

Another reason to have a long term core position in the stock market is that it can provide diversity. At the beginning of 2013 as

I write this chapter, the stock market has made new highs nine days in a row. Volatility and range are very narrow. Our stock index day trading systems have gone long on some pullbacks but the nature of this type of bull market does not generate many trades and our trading frequency is much lower this year in 2013.

Going broke taking profits as a day trader

If you are a day trader, short term trader, or system trader, you absolutely need the bigger winners to make up for losing trades and transaction costs. If it were possible to have 100% winners then you could take quick profits on every trade and ignore what I am about to say. Good luck coming up with a strategy that has 100% winners!

When testing Gap Fill and Reverse on Crude Oil we can get 91% profitable trades with a $50 profit target but the average profit per trade before any transaction costs is only $4. If you then add a $5 commission, this strategy becomes a losing strategy without even considering slippage. This type of approach can draw in novice traders with the feeling of frequent success, only to end up in the negative with the big losers. Many retail traders with a "high frequency" personality will succumb to the tight profit target and big stop loss approach when trading on a discretionary basis. Because there are so many more winners and only an occasional big loser, it is difficult to adjust and see the occasional big loser for what it is. It just feels like really bad luck that will never happen again, after all, we are right 90% of the time!

The concept of using a stop loss and letting your profits run is a universal trading concept that has been around a long time and the research data for many trading systems continues to prove that this principle gives us the best chance for being profitable. Micromanaging your trades with tight stop losses, profit targets, trailing stop losses, and breakeven stop losses will usually generate a losing strategy in real trading.

Don't churn your own account by choking your strategy to death!

The same principal is true on manual trades or discretionary trading. For most strategies and markets, using a stop loss smaller than $300 per contract as well as putting in a tight profit target will not allow us to generate enough profits over time to make up for losses and transaction costs.

Tight stop losses can generate many losing trades. Using tight stop losses can actually be a good approach as long as you have a good entry and you let your winners "run". We have strategies that are only 30 - 40% profitable with "tight" $300 stop losses per contract that have worked very well for us. We do not want to limit profits by placing a tight profit target just to increase accuracy. When trading multiple systems or multiple contracts per system we can use this approach (of adding profit targets) on some contracts for a diversity of exits as there are choppy trading periods in narrow ranging markets where profit targets will work better for an extended period of time and the returns can be more consistent.

The next image is the Tradestation Performance Summary for Gap Fill and Reverse with a $50 profit target and no slippage or commission. The high percentage of accuracy can be seen at 91% and the low average trade profit is only $4. After slippage and commission is taken out of this strategy there would still a high percentage of winners but a losing strategy at best.

Tradestation Performance Summary

Chart created on Tradestation, the flagship product of Tradestation Technologies

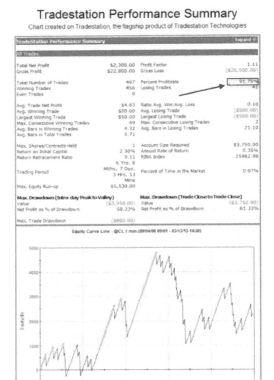

Figure 12-1

For many traders, having a trading system that matches their trading psychology is critical to staying with the system. Trading with no profit target or having less than 50% winners and watching the strategy give back significant profits makes it difficult for many beginning traders to continue trading the system. If this is the case, it is better to opt for a strategy with a profit target, even if the overall return is lower than to abandon the trading system for a more un-proven trading method. If this is the approach that you choose, be sure to select a strategy with a profit target that is still high enough to generate a high enough average trade profit to adequately overcome slippage and commission.

The point of this chapter is that profit targets are not bad but typically need to be much higher than most new traders realize. Additionally, a strategy that has a high percentage of winning trades is not necessarily a good strategy if it also has the big loser that is 10 times larger than the profit target, and has a small average trade profit that will not overcome slippage and commission. The conclusion may then become, "Why not have the best of both worlds and develop a trading system that is both highly accurate (such as 90%+) and also has a high average trade profit?" This approaches "holy grail" territory and the realm of impossibility as it would require the market to become extremely inefficient or very easy to trade. It is possible to develop a system with these sort of statistics but the strategies I have found with these hypothetical results do not have enough trades to be statistically significant (and trade very rarely), are on a very small period of data, and/or are highly optimized on a small period of data and will not work in the future.

I have not found the "holy grail" trading system that would generate 10 trades per day, have 90% profitability and average $100 per trade per contract over a significant period of time.

It is important to realistically test your trading system to make sure that it works and will still be profitable after slippage and commission.

In **Chapter 15 Testing Different Entry Techniques & Learning Code** we show how to trade a multi-contract strategy that provides the best of both worlds as we develop a multicontract version of the Gap Fill and Reverse trading system and show how half of the contracts can use a profit target and the other half can be held until the end of the day.

13.   How Stop Losses Affect Trading Performance

You can go broke with stop losses that are too tight.

One of the most important aspects of trading is risk management. There can be a big misunderstanding among traders of how risk management should work when trading the markets. Many traders switch between analysis based on percentage of capital and analysis based on dollar amount. Many traders may learn from books that proper risk management based on large or institutional traders will limit risk on a per trade basis to 1-2% while others may risk less than 1/2% per trade. A new trader opening up a $10,000 account will translate this to mean that their stop losses should be between $50 and $200 per futures contract per trade.

After nearly 20 years of studying the markets, pinpointing trades to use stop losses this tight (based on trading futures contracts) is rarely successful. I find that this approach does not allow enough room for many trades to work so you can risk a small amount per trade and be wrong 90% of the time.

In this scenario, when we set tight stop losses, we are asking the market to conform to our account size and stop loss preferences of risk per trade instead of taking a realistic view at how the market moves and choosing a stop loss that will work in the current market conditions.

As traders we have to test our strategies against the market and then provide the adequate amount of capital needed to trade the strategy. If the stop loss or risk for our trading system is too big as a percentage of account size then more capital needs to be allocated to our trading account, if available, instead of tightening the stop loss and hoping the market conforms to untested strategies and unrealistic approaches. As always, there is an exception for every scenario and it is possible that some may have a successful trading system with tight stop losses.

An example of how tight stop losses affect our trading systems, we will take a look at a range of stop losses in the Gap Fill German

Bund trading system between 100 and 500 Euros. The Tradestation Performance Summaries for each are shown below.

TradeStation Performance Summary

All Trades

Total Net Profit	€950.00	Profit Factor	1.05
Gross Profit	€18,150.00	Gross Loss	(€17,300.00)
Total Number of Trades	276	Percent Profitable	36.23%
Winning Trades	100	Losing Trades	175
Even Trades	1		
Avg. Trade Net Profit	€3.08	Ratio Avg. Win:Avg. Loss	1.84
Avg. Winning Trade	€181.50	Avg. Losing Trade	(€98.86)
Largest Winning Trade	€200.00	Largest Losing Trade	(€100.00)
Max. Consecutive Winning Trades	4	Max. Consecutive Losing Trades	8
Avg. Bars in Winning Trades	102.39	Avg. Bars in Losing Trades	55.31
Avg. Bars in Total Trades	73.02		
Max. Shares/Contracts Held	1	Account Size Required	€1,950.00
Return on Initial Capital	0.85%	Annual Rate of Return	0.22%
Return Retracement Ratio	0.11	RINA Index	1048.02
Trading Period	3 Yrs, 10 Mths, 24 Dys, 13 Hrs, 6 Mins	Percent of Time in the Market	1.00%
Max. Equity Run-up	€3,260.00		

Max. Drawdown (Intra-day Peak to Valley)		Max. Drawdown (Trade Close to Trade Close)	
Value	(€2,130.00)	Value	(€1,953.00)
Net Profit as % of Drawdown	40.28%	Net Profit as % of Drawdown	43.59%
Max. Trade Drawdown	(€100.00)		

Equity Curve Line - @FGBL 1 min.(06/01/09 02:02 - 04/26/13 16:00)

100 Euro Stop Loss

Figure 13-1

Chart created by Tradestation, the flaship product of Tradestation Technologies

Figure 13-2

Figure 13-3

Chart created by Tradestation, the flagship product of Tradestation Technologies

TradeStation Performance Summary			Expand ≢
All Trades			
Total Net Profit	€14,240.00	Profit Factor	1.91
Gross Profit	€29,830.00	Gross Loss	(€15,590.00)
Total Number of Trades	276	Percent Profitable	65.22%
Winning Trades	180	Losing Trades	92
Even Trades	4		
Avg. Trade Net Profit	€51.59	Ratio Avg. Win:Avg. Loss	0.98
Avg. Winning Trade	€165.72	Avg. Losing Trade	(€169.46)
Largest Winning Trade	€200.00	Largest Losing Trade	(€400.00)
Max. Consecutive Winning Trades	12	Max. Consecutive Losing Trades	4
Avg. Bars in Winning Trades	132.12	Avg. Bars in Losing Trades	216.55
Avg. Bars in Total Trades	161.72		
Max. Shares/Contracts Held	1	Account Size Required	€1,310.00
Return on Initial Capital	14.24%	Annual Rate of Return	3.41%
Return Retracement Ratio	0.36	RINA Index	4166.77
Trading Period	0 Yrs, 10 Mths, 24 Dys, 13 Hrs, 6 Mins	Percent of Time in the Market	2.22%
Max. Equity Run-up	€15,170.00		

Max. Drawdown (Intra-day Peak to Valley)		Max. Drawdown (Trade Close to Trade-Close)	
Value	(€1,550.00)	Value	(€1,310.00)
Net Profit as % of Drawdown	918.71%	Net Profit as % of Drawdown	1087.02%
Max. Trade Drawdown	(€400.00)		

Equity Curve Line - @FGBL 1 min.(06/01/09 02:02 - 04/29/10 16:00)

400 Euro
Stop Loss

Figure 13-4

207

Chart created by Tradestation, the flagship product of Tradestation Technologies

Figure 13-5

From each of the Tradestation Performance Summaries, we see
that the performance improves as we increase the stop loss and
give the strategy enough room to work. The Net Profit as a % of
Drawdown and Average Trade Net Profit continues to increase
as we increase the stop loss. In this case the 100 Euro Stop Loss
shows a small gain but once we add slippage and commission to
this strategy, the 100 Euro Stop Loss version will end up

208

showing a net loss since the average trade profit is only 3.08 Euros.

What we learn from this is that a tighter stop loss actually increases the risk since we end up taking trades that don't work out to our advantage. The risk per trade is small but the risk to our account is large and we will effectively churn our own account size down slowly. Even though this is just one example, I find this principle and these results to be universal across most trading systems and even manual or discretionary approaches. Using a tight stop loss based on the fear of losing too much on any given trade, is actually more risky than using a larger stop loss on a strategy that actually gives us an edge and opportunity to be profitable.

There is truth in the saying that "Scared money doesn't make money". As traders we have to accept a reasonable amount of risk on each trade. This is the exact opposite psychology and mindset of traders who take risks that are too large and let losses get too big.

Gap Fill German Bund is one of those strategies that work better with a tighter profit target. This can be the case for many countertrend trading systems. If we increase the profit target for this trading system, then the strategy does not perform as well. This particular trading system is based on a short term time frame and is looking for a very small reactionary move based on the time period that this market has been closed from its previous day's trading session.

14.   Multiple Exit Strategies

This chapter discusses how to exit trades by developing a trading strategy that has different exit points. In this type of strategy we will exit half of our position using a profit target and the other half at the end of the day. A stop loss will also be used. We will use the Gap Fill and Reverse trading system on Crude Oil to demonstrate how to set up and program this type of strategy. This will allow us to see the combined results of what we have developed in the Gap Fill and Reverse trading strategy for Crude Oil based on what we have discussed in previous chapters about the effects of profit targets.

We will show how to write code to test a multiple contract strategy with two different exit strategies in both Tradestation and NinjaTrader. The open code is very valuable and can be modified by more experienced programmers to continue to customize this strategy. The strategy development will begin by using a $500 profit target for the first half of our contracts (or 50 points in Crude Oil) while the remaining half of our position will exit at the end of the day in order to allow our position the opportunity to let profits run. The initial stop loss will be $500 or 50 points per contract. The image below demonstrates a short trade in Crude Oil on September 17, 2015 in NinjaTrader.

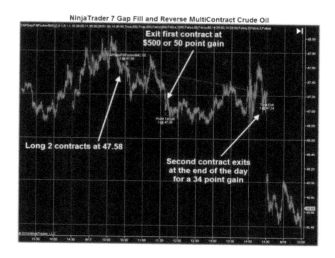

Figure 14-1

This strategy uses the same custom session that we used in **Chapter 6** on one minute bars from 9:00am - 2:30pm EST during the pit or open outcry session. In NinjaTrader the Custom Session is the Nymex Energy RTH.

We take a look at the inputs below and notice that we use most of the same inputs that we used in **Chapter 6** in **Figure 6-18**. The cntrcts input (representing the number of contracts to trade) should be an even number since we exit half of the contracts at the profit target. The profit target input has changed and has been set to True.

Figure 14-2

We show the hypothetical results from the NinjaTrader platform next and discuss the results. A good way to measure the results of this strategy is to take a look at the results for the single contract strategy that we developed without a profit target and multiply the results times two since we are now using two contracts.

Gap Fill and Reverse Crude Oil MultiContract Trading System with Limit Orders Performance Summary in NinjaTrader 7

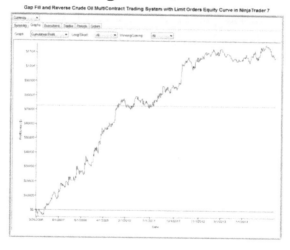

Figure 14-3

Gap Fill and Reverse Crude Oil MultiContract Trading System with Limit Orders Equity Curve in NinjaTrader 7

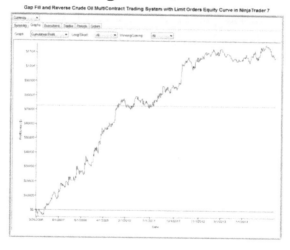

Figure 14-4

The drawdown is less than 2 times as much as the single contract version but the Total Net Profit is also smaller than two

213

times the single contract version (we multiply times two since we trade 2 contracts in this version compared to 1 contract in the original development). The real benefit in taking this approach is the Percent Profitable increases from 45% in the single contract version to 61% in the multi-contract version with the profit target. This is in reference to the NinjaTrader Performance Report in **Figure 6-19**.

The maximum number of consecutive winning trades more than doubles in the multi-contract version. It may not be within a trader's trading psychology to trade a strategy that has the best absolute hypothetical return if percent profitability drops below a certain level. Some traders do not care and let the system work and can handle low percentage profitability while others feel the need for more short term successes. If this is the case in your trading psychology, you will need to focus on strategies above 5060% profitability even if the absolute total return is lower than strategies that do not use a profit target.

The next image shows us the data and input settings for NinjaTrader. Studying the code in this book and experimenting is one of the best ways to learn how to customize and code your own strategies. **The NinjaScript and Tradestation code can be downloaded from our website. See Chapter 16 to learn how to do this.**

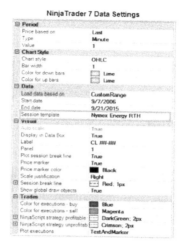

Figure 14-5

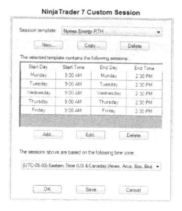

Figure 14-6

The main coding difference is how we modify the profit target section of the code. We determine that if the number of contracts currently being traded is the same number of contracts that we entered the trade with(Position.Quantity == _cntrcts), then we sell half of the contracts (Position.Quantity/2) at our profit target.

Setting up the Strategy in Tradestation

In this section we show the setup for Tradestation with a series of images including an example long trade, input settings, performance report, data settings, and custom session.

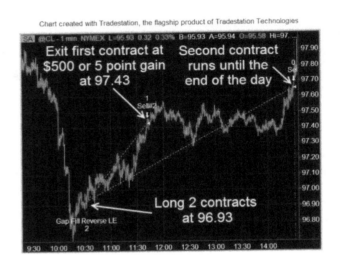

Figure 14-7

Figure 14-8

217

Figure 14-9

218

Figure 14-10

Figure 14-11

Testing Trading Systems around Holidays and Early Closings

We like to use the statement SetExitonClose to exit any trades that may occur during a holiday shortened session where the actual market closes and data stops before the end of our regular session. This scenario is more common for half days where the stock market closes early. On these days, the E-mini S&P will stop trading at 12:15 pm CST before a holiday and any trades that are left open would exit on the close of the last bar during a back test if SetExitonClose was used since the typical exit time that is later in the afternoon would never occur for that day. As traders, it is important to know in advance about early closings in order to make a decision to either not trade on these days or to manually exit a few seconds before the close so that your trades will match hypothetical results. It is also possible to modify code for a strategy to automatically exit at an earlier time before the earlier close occurs.

For example if the market had an early close on 12/24/2012 and we knew the early closing was at 12:15 pm, we could add the following code to the strategy.

If Date=ELDate(12,24,2012) and Time=1214 Then Sell Next Bar at market;
If Date=ELDate(12,24,2012) and Time=1214 Then Buy to Cover Next Bar at market;

The first line would exit any long trades and the second line would exit any short trades. It is also very important to understand that this is for one minute charts since a timestamp of 1214 would occur only on a one minute chart (not taking into consideration tick charts or other types of charts). One minute charts have a time stamp for each minute and each minute can be referenced. If five minute bars are being used, for example, then the timestamp occurs only every 5 minutes and only 5 minute intervals can be referenced and the code may look like this:

If Date=ELDate(12,24,2012) and Time=1210 Then Sell Next Bar at market;
If Date=ELDate(12,24,2012) and Time=1210 Then Buy to Cover Next Bar at market;

The only difference between the two sets of code is based on the time change in the code from 1214 to 1210. If fifteen minute bars were used, then 1200 would be the time to reference. We like to develop strategies on the smallest timeframe possible so that we can reference each minute and more accurately back test strategies for situations such as these.

The goal of system trading, besides trading profitably, is to closely match in real time the results that we achieve during a back test. The automation setup should very closely match the way the strategy was back tested and the walk forward results. When using a statement such as SetExitonClose to back test a strategy and to make sure that early session closes show exits on hypothetical backrests and trades were not held until the market, re-opened, the exit will take place at the closing price of the last bar of the day. This is difficult and impossible to implement for automation since a trade cannot be sent once the market is closed. To match the results closely, a manual exit a few seconds before the close or to program the strategy to not trade on holidays or half days (sometimes markets such as the E-mini S&P are open for the first hour or more even when the stock market is closed - we don't trade on these days but your signal might generate a trade if it is not programmed to not trade on these days) is the most accurate way to match real time trading to back testing and forward testing. It is also accurate on one minute intervals to write the code that we showed above where the exit automatically takes place one minute before the close. It is less accurate, when applying this to a larger time interval based strategy since the earlier you exit before the actual close of the day the more time difference occurs between exiting 15 minutes before the close on 15 minute interval bars and then comparing the results to a back test that uses SetExitonClose (which exits at the close of the last bar). On 15 minute bars, the implementation would occur 15 minutes before an exit of a future back test that uses the statement SetExitOnClose.

The code that we discussed in this section could be left in the strategy, instead of just adding it or changing it for each holiday, (therefore creating a list of early closing dates and times) so that the back test in the future would accurately represent what you were doing in real trading. If this is the approach that will be taken, it is important to go back and find all early closings and implement this in the back test so that it will be known how exiting at an earlier time before an early close would affect the strategy.

For example, the stock market was closed on 10/29-10/30 in 2012 for Hurricane Sandy. Going back more than a decade, the stock market was closed for about a week after 9/11/2001. These are two events where it was unknown that the stock market would be closed on these days in advance. All future holiday schedules are also not known when the strategy is developed so dates for early closes could be adjusted in the code as holidays come up.

Often times when you look at a back test you may see a largest losing trade or largest winning trade bigger than the stop loss or profit target. This can be the case if a strategy is tested on days where the market closes early and the exit time of the strategy would occur after the market closed. Since the market is closed, the strategy does not exit and will still be in a trade when the market re-opens. As we know, markets can open at much different prices from their close and this can create that largest losing trade or largest winning trade that is bigger than the stop loss or profit target. Adding SetExitonClose can usually resolve it since it will generate an exit on the close of the last bar of the day.

Once you add that SetExitonClose to your strategy, it may improve or hurt your strategy as holding positions overnight on a strategy that was intended to be a day trade strategy can sometimes improve the strategy by creating a longer holding period while other strategies may have worse results based on overnight gaps that are adverse to the direction of the trade.

Once you do add the SetExitOnClose and see how all of the holiday shortened sessions close trades at the end of the day on your back test, you may then decide to implement a particular strategy that uses the results of the SetExitOnClose. To do this, you will need to manually exit right at the close on those trading sessions that close early. It is important to pay attention to the details of this section so that there is not a big distortion between what can be achieved in real trading versus hypothetical results.

15. Testing Different Entry Techniques & Learning Code

In this chapter we take a look at how to test different trend filters used for our entry technique within one trading system. We answer the question of how do we code a strategy to optimize different rule sets. In our book, "Seven Trading Systems for the S&P Futures" we used the 100 day moving average to determine the trend. What if we have multiple ideas for determining the trend and would like to add all of these ideas to the strategy to test which trend determination method works best by running the optimization tool. This method could help us more quickly determine the best way to trade a market or a group of different markets.

We will take a look at five different trend rules and the programming structure for our code so that we can apply these rules to any other strategy. For more advanced traders and programmers, you can use this coding structure to add additional rules. We will apply these rules to the Gap Fill and Reverse trading system and test each rule separately. Some of the rules will improve the strategy and other rule's will not improve this particular strategy but may improve other types of strategies. The code can be added to any existing open code strategy and tested.

The five trend based rules that we will test are:

225

1.) Test the current price against the previous day's close. The previous day's close will have an input for testing against number of days back. For this particular strategy, we want to go long when it penetrates the previous day's close so the look back for testing against previous days closes should be more than 1. For longs we want to be above the L1 daily closes ago and for shorts, we want to be below L1 daily closes ago.

2.) Test the daily stochastic to see if it is above the overbought threshold for longs or below the oversold threshold for shorts.

3.) Test the current price against the exponential moving average. For longs, we want to be above the exponential moving average and for shorts we want to be below the exponential moving average.

4.) Test the Tick Low and Tick Highs of the current day. For longs we want the NYSE TICK to stay above a set Tick Low value (set as an input) and for shorts we want the NYSE TICK to stay below a set Tick High value (set as an input).

5.) Test the spread between the NYSE ADVANCERS and

NYSE DECLINERS. For longs; we want the spread to be above the buy threshold and for shorts; we want the spread to be below the sell threshold.

The first rule is a basic trend concept of buying when the current price is above the close of L1 days ago for longs and below the close of L1 days ago for shorts.

The second rule uses stochastics based on the daily bars or data2 in the chart window and goes long when the daily stochastics is overbought and goes short when the daily stochastics is oversold. This is a contrarian concept as we have found many times that when the daily bars are in the overbought zone then there can be a continued short term bid moving prices higher and when the daily bars are in the oversold zone then there can be a continued short term offer moving prices lower. Keep in mind these are very short term trades and are not long term trading techniques for capturing a longer term trends.

The third rule uses the exponential moving average to determine the trend. Moving averages are one of the oldest trend techniques. When used alone, I find that they rarely work. Combining them with a pattern and additional rules can be very powerful.

The fourth rule uses a market internal called the NYSE TICK. This rule only makes sense on stock index futures but can potentially be used on non-stock index futures markets if its correlation to the stock index futures is close to 100%.

The NYSE TICK keeps track of the number of stocks on the New York Stock Exchange that are in an uptick minus those in a downtick. In a bullish trend, the NYSE TICK will remain mostly above 0 and will typically see higher and more positive TICK values than negative TICK values. In a bearish trend, the NYSE TICK will typically see lower negative NYSE TICK values than higher NYSE TICK values.

The NYSE TICK is different than actual market prices since it can have both positive and negative values. On any given day, the NYSE TICK can typically see readings above +1000 and below 1000. The NYSE TICK tracks approximately 3700 stocks. When there is a +1000 TICK reading, it means that there are 1000 more stocks in an uptick than in a downtick. When there is a -1000 TICK reading, it means that there are 1000 more stocks in a downtick than in an uptick. An uptick means that the current price is higher than the previous price while a downtick means that the current price is lower than the previous price.

The default values that we use in our code is to take long entries if the TICK Low is not below -500 and we can take short entries if the TICK High is not above +500. The reason that we allow the TICK to still have negative numbers for longs and positive numbers for shorts is because it is a very "fluid" indicator that quickly moves between positive and negative numbers and we are willing to go long if the TICK isn't "too negative" and are willing to go short if the TICK isn't "too positive".

Below is a chart of the NYSE TICK on one minute bars in the Tradestation Platform.

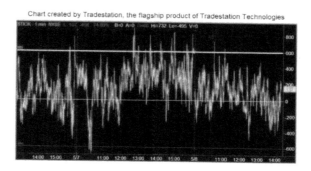

Chart created by Tradestation, the flagship product of Tradestation Technologies

Figure 15-1

The chart includes the +600 line shown in blue, the -600 line shown in red, and the 0 line shown in yellow. These thresholds are highlighted and shown for trading on May 7 and 8th with a one minute chart. The vertical red lines represent the start and stop of each day's session. During the current timeframe during the writing of this book (2013), the market has had very low volatility and narrow ranges in the stock index futures. The ranges of the NYSE TICK have been very low during this current timeframe as well so we have used +/-600 as the thresholds for this example.

The symbol for the NYSE TICK in Tradestation is $TICK. For other platforms and data providers the symbol will be different. The NYSE TICK and other types of market internals are also different from price since they are calculated by the data provider instead of by the exchange. Different data providers can update the prices at different time intervals (in the millisecond to second range) with some providers having more delays than others. This generates different high and low values for market internals such as the NYSE TICK and NYSE ADVANCERS and DECLINERS (which we will discuss next). When using different platforms or different data feeds, this concept should be kept in mind as adjustments may be needed in the threshold parameters for TICK, ADVANCERS, and DECLINERS to generate the same results between platforms.

The fifth rule uses the NYSE ADVANCERS and NYSE DECLINERS, which are also market internals. This rule is similar to the previous rule since it only makes sense on stock index futures but can potentially be used on non-stock index futures markets if its correlation to the stock index futures is close to 100%.

The NYSE ADVANCERS keeps track of the number of stocks on the New York Stock Exchange that are above their previous day's close. The NYSE DECLINERS keeps track of the number of stocks on the New York Stock Exchange that are below their previous day's close.

In rule five we take the difference between the NYSE ADVANCERS and NYSE DECLINERS to get an oscillator value that is similar to the NYSE TICK in that the number created by the difference in these two values can move between +1000 (or higher) and -1000 and lower. These numbers do not change as quickly as the NYSE TICK since they are tracking the progress of stocks based on yesterday's close while the NYSE TICK is updated based on the previous price or tick that is updated tick by tick on all individual stocks.

In the next image we show a chart of the NYSE ADVANCERS as data1 shown as the green data, NYSE DECLINERS as data2 shown as the orange data, with the spread difference between them shown with a blue line with the latest value of +165. In Tradestation the symbol for NYSE ADVANCERS is $ADV while the symbol for NYSE DECLINERS is $DECL.

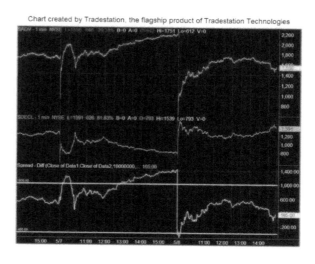

Figure 15-2

231

There is another market internal provided by Tradestation that is represented as the $ADD. This one data stream will show the difference between the ADVANCERS and DECLINERS and will not only just give us the closing price of the calculated spread but also the Open, High, and Low for the interval we are interested in. The $ADD has less history than the $ADV and $DECL so more historical back testing can achieved when using the $ADV and $DECL.

The chart below shows a plot of the $ADD. Notice the difference between the bars with Open, High, Low, Close values versus a straight line spread calculation based on the close of each interval. In order to see the resolution of each one minute bar, there is only a two hour window on the chart. The zero line is drawn with a yellow horizontal bar.

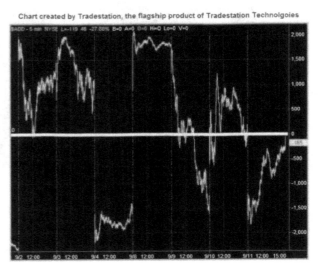

Chart created by Tradestation, the flagship product of Tradestation Technolgoies

Figure 15-3

Now that we have defined the individual trend rules we will incorporate them into our original Gap Fill and Reverse trading system and then analyze how each rule affects a trading systems performance.

Programming the Code

In this section of the Chapter we talk about programming the code for this type of strategy. This is more technical and can be skipped by those who do not plan on programming their own strategies.

When I started out, I had a technical background in engineering but was still far from being an expert programmer. Today I am pretty good at the basics of programming. I consider myself a market person with average programming skills and hire programmers for the more complex coding. I still like to spend most of my time studying the markets rather than studying every nuance of writing code. It is not practical for me, even when I hire programmers to not know some of the basics or have an understanding of basic coding.

When I first started I read many books with example code to learn what I have learned today. I pay it forward in this book as the code is revealed in this section as well as a detailed explanation of what each block of code does. When I first started, I found examples like this very useful in learning how to develop my own trading systems. Understanding the details of the logic of the code for a trading system can help understand the details of the market and a trading system.

It is not practical for most traders starting out to hire a programmer to test every idea they have. This can become very expensive since most new, as well as experienced traders will have ideas that do not work. Making market observations and finding what is true in the market can take time. Over 90% of my ideas about the market still do not work well. Over 90% of indicator based ideas that I see being promoted do not work well when I program these indicator based rules into a strategy. It is possible that those who are promoting various indicator based ideas to be profitable traders and that their idea works for them as a discretionary trader and some of their followers. Discretionary methods are very difficult to replicate exactly and the results can vary greatly between traders. Setting it up in an automated trading system is the best way to communicate the specifics of the trading approach that you are using and to see the real truth of the strategy versus a discretionary method.

If you have an indicator with a specific set of rules, why not create a system and test it to see how it holds up? **Sometimes the truth can ruin our hopes.** It took me five years of research before I had a system that I really trusted! Most of my ideas were exactly wrong and the opposite (reversing the buy and sell short signals) of my initial ideas were actually more profitable. To me this proves the counter intuitive nature of the markets and trading and what makes manual or discretionary trading more difficult than using a trading system for most traders.

It is good to have some basic programming skills in order to study basic market patterns on your own and to develop proprietary ideas without sharing them. Once the basic strategy has been developed and there is a known idea, fine tuning it with a programmer is an approach that can be taken.

The programming methods used in this section are some of the methods that I use in multiple strategy development for strategies that test and use multiple rules. These methods will allow us to turn different trend trading rules on or off with 1's and 0's (as trading system inputs). This type of programming method is used in some of my other strategies such as my money management algorithms.

The way we incorporate multiple methods into our code is to create a condition for each rule for both the long and short entries. We turn the rule "On' by using a 1 and turn it "Off" by using a 0. This allows us to use the optimization tool by testing the rules and turning them On and Off during optimization by optimizing each rule from 0 to 1 with an increment of 1. We could use True or False but the optimization tool does not optimize True/False inputs at the time of this writing (but may in the future, typing 1 or 0 is quicker than typing True and False). Simply stated, 1 means the rule is True and "On" while 0 means the rule is False and "Off".

This is Boolean logic for those familiar with this concept.

In order to use these rules together in one statement we set each Trend Rule to its condition for trending if the Trend Rule is True, causing the strategy to check for the truth of the rule and if it is False, we set the Trend Rule to True so it won't check for the truth of the rule. For example, the first trend Rule is TrendRule1. The code for this condition looks like this.

If   TrendRule1=1   Then
Condition1=Close>CloseD(TrendRule_L1);
If TrendRule<>1 Then Condition1=True;

We have 10 sets of rules, five for the long side and five for the short side.

We change the entry code section for the long side from the original Gap Fill and Reverse trading system in the EasyLanguage below:

EasyLanguage Code in Tradestation, the flagship product of Tradestation Technologies

```
22   If Time>StartTime and Time<FinishTime
23       and EntriesToday(Date)<MaxDailyEntries
24       and Op>Cl+GapSize
25       and Close< Cl-PenetrationPts
26       Then Buy ("Gap Fill Rev LE") cntrcts contracts
27           Next Bar at Close + PTS Stop;
```

236

Figure 15-4

The modified EasyLanguage code for the long side which includes the five conditions for the long side is shown below:

```
EasyLanguage Code in Tradestation, the flagship product of Tradestation Technologies
87    If Time>StartTime and Time<FinishTime
88          and EntriesToday(Date)<MaxDailyEntries
89          and Op>Cl+GapSize
90          And Close < Cl-PenetrationPts
91          and Condition1
92          and Condition2
93          and Condition3
94          and Condition4
95          and Condition5
96          Then Buy ("Gap Fill Rev ME LE") cntrcts contracts
97             Next Bar at Close + PTS Stop;
```

Figure 15-5

This programming method works well. If TrendRule1 through TrendRule5 is set to 0 or False, then Condition1 through Condition5 is automatically True and the strategy will match the original strategy since it will not require TrendRule1 through TrendRule5 to have any conditions met for the strategy to be True. Condition1 through Condition5 only have requirements that need to be met if the TrendRule1 through TrendRule5 is set to 1 or True.

The advantage of writing the code this way is that multiple trend rules can be combined. If TrendRule1 is set to 1 and TrendRule2 is set to 1 then only the two rules related to those trend rules will be checked and the other trend rules will be ignored.

We will now show the rest of the code in separate sections so that we can provide an actual summary of the code for each section. The first section includes the inputs and comments. Comments appear in green and have a // at the beginning of each line. Any line that starts with a // will be ignored by Tradestation EasyLanguage when calculating the strategy. Comments can be useful for adding notes or to remove sections of the code for testing to see how removing parts of the code would affect a strategy.

The lines we have added are boxed in green and include the TrendRule1 through TrendRule10 inputs to set each Rule to 0 or 1 which is True or False. There are inputs for each of the TrendRules as well. With these inputs, each of the rules can be turned On or Off and with each rule, we can also change some of the inputs related to the rules.

```
1  // ***Copyright (c) 1995-2019 Capstone Trading Systems All rights reserved. **
2  // Gap Fill and Reverse (aka Gap Fill Fade) trading system with MultiEntry and Stops
3  // Data1 is E-mini S&P, 1 minute chart
4  // Data2 is E-mini S&P, Daily chart
5  // Data3 is NYSE TICK
6  // Data4 is NYSE Advancers
7  // Data5 is NYSE Decliners
8
9  // Data1 and Data2 can be any other market as well such as
10 //    Euro Currency, DAX, Crude, SPY, IWM, NQDAL, etc
11
12 Inputs: cntrcts(1),
13     GapSize(2), PenetrationPts(2), PTS(.5),
14     MaxDailyEntries(1), StartTime(930), FinishTime(1530),
15     TrendRule1(0),
16     TrendRule2(0),
17     TrendRule3(0),
18     TrendRule4(0),
19     TrendRule5(0),
20     TrendRule6(0),
21     TrendRule7(0),
22     TrendRule8(0),
23     TrendRule9(0),
24     TrendRule10(0),
25     TrendRule1_L1(9),
26     TrendRule2_L1(14),
27     TrendRule3_StochHigh(40),
28     TrendRule3_L1(12),
29     TrendRule4_TickLow(-500),
30     TrendRule5_mvcl(600),
31     TrendRule6_L1(3),
32     TrendRule7_L1(14),
33     TrendRule7_StochLow(20),
34     TrendRule8_L1(12),
35     TrendRule9_TickHigh(500),
36     TrendRule10_mvcl(-600),
37     StpLs(True), StpLsAmt(650),
38     PrfTg(True), PrfTgAmt(900),
39     BreakEven(False), BreakEvenAmt(500),
40     DollarTrail(False), DollarTrailAmt(1000),
41     BarsSinceEntryExitLongs(False), BarsToExitLongs(60),
42     BarsSinceEntryExitShorts(False), BarsToExitShorts(60),
43     LongExTime(1610), ShortExTime(1610);
```

Figure 15-6

In the next section of the code we include our Vars or variables and the definition for the day's Open, Close, and starting Time.

```
45  Vars: Tim(0), Op(0), C1(0), Op2(0), C12(0);
46
47  If Date<>Date[1] Then Tim=Time;
48  If Date<>Date[1] Then Op=Open;
49  If Date<>Date[1] Then C1=Close[1];
```

Figure 15-7

In this section we "anchor" values for the Open of the current session and the Close of the previous session by setting Op to the Open at the beginning of the session by referencing the first

239

bar of the session based on a change in calendar date and by setting Cl to the Close of the previous day using the same method. The Op and Cl relationships are used later in the code to define the Gap and to test if the Gap is large enough to take the trade.

The next image is the Long Trend Trade Setups.

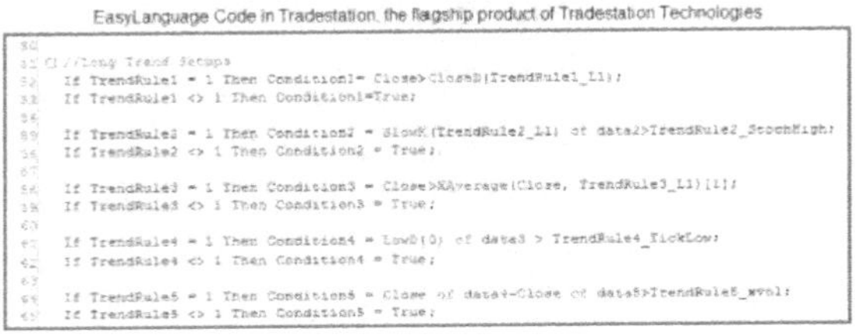
EasyLanguage Code in Tradestation, the flagship product of Tradestation Technologies

```
//Long Trend Setups
  If TrendRule1 = 1 Then Condition1= Close>CloseD(TrendRule1_L1);
  If TrendRule1 <> 1 Then Condition1=True;

  If TrendRule2 = 1 Then Condition2 = SlowK(TrendRule2_L1) of data2>TrendRule2_StochHigh;
  If TrendRule2 <> 1 Then Condition2 = True;

  If TrendRule3 = 1 Then Condition3 = Close>XAverage(Close, TrendRule3_L1)[1];
  If TrendRule3 <> 1 Then Condition3 = True;

  If TrendRule4 = 1 Then Condition4 = LowD(0) of data3 > TrendRule4_TickLow;
  If TrendRule4 <> 1 Then Condition4 = True;

  If TrendRule5 = 1 Then Condition5 = Close of data4-Close of data5>TrendRule5_avol;
  If TrendRule5 <> 1 Then Condition5 = True;
```

Figure 15-8

We see each of the TrendRules that we defined at the beginning of this chapter. If any of the TrendRules (TrendRule1 - TrendRule5) are set to 1, then they are assigned a Condition with a rule. If any of the Trend Rules are set to a number other than 1, then the Conditions are automatically set to True and the associated trend rule will not be checked. There are inputs for each Trend Rule to set to 1 or 0 and there are inputs related to each of the Trend Rules. Trend Rule 1 uses a look back period for the number of days to check against the current close to see if the current close is higher than the Close, TrendRule1_L1 day's ago.

TrendRule2_L1 and TrendRule2_StochHigh are the look back period for the stochastic calculation of the daily bars requiring the stochastic to be above TrendRule2_StochHigh threshold value. The default look back is 14 and the StochHigh threshold is 80.

TrendRule3_L1 is the look back period for the exponential moving average to compare to the current price.

TrendRule4_TickLow is the TickLow threshold that defaults to 500. As long as the low of the NYSE TICK is above -500 for the day then the trend is still up.

TrendRule5_xvol is the threshold of the spread between the NYSE ADVANCERS and NYSE DECLINERS and defaults to 600 for long trades. There must be 600 more NYSE stocks up for the day than down for the day.

The next image is the Short Trend Setups.

EasyLanguage Code in Tradestation, the flagship product of Tradestation Technologies

```
//Short Trend Setups
    If TrendRule6 = 1 Then Condition6= Close<CloseD(TrendRule6_L1);
    If TrendRule6 <> 1 Then Condition6=True;

    If TrendRule7 = 1 Then Condition7 = SlowK(TrendRule7_L1) of data2<TrendRule7_StochLow;
    If TrendRule7 <> 1 Then Condition7 = True;

    If TrendRule8 = 1 Then Condition8 = Close<XAverage(Close, TrendRule8_L1)[1];
    If TrendRule8 <> 1 Then Condition8 = True;

    If TrendRule9 = 1 Then Condition9 = HighD(0) of data3 < TrendRule9_TickHigh;
    If TrendRule9 <> 1 Then Condition9 = True;

    If TrendRule10 = 1 Then Condition10 = Close of data4-Close of data5<TrendRule10_xvol;
    If TrendRule10 <> 1 Then Condition10 = True;
```

Figure 15-9

The short entry Trend Rules are TrendRule6 - TrendRule10. The short side is similar to the long side with the trend requirements being in the opposite direction.

The next image is the list of Entry Rules for long and short trades.

EasyLanguage Code in Tradestation, the flagship product of Tradestation Technologies

```
83  □ //Entry Rules
84
85     If Time>StartTime and Time<FinishTime
86        and EntriesToday(Date)<MaxDailyEntries
87        and Op>Cl-GapSize
88        And Close < Cl-PenetrationPts
89        and Condition1
90        and Condition2
91        and Condition3
92        and Condition4
93        and Condition5
94        Then Buy ("Gap Fill Rev ME LE") cntrcts contracts
95              Next Bar at Close + PTS Stop;
96
97     If Time>StartTime and Time<FinishTime
98        and EntriesToday(Date)<MaxDailyEntries
99        and Op<Cl-GapSize
100       And Close > Cl+PenetrationPts
101       and Condition6
102       and Condition7
103       and Condition8
104       and Condition9
105       and Condition10
106       Then Sell Short ("Gap Fill Rev ME SE") cntrcts contracts
107             Next Bar at Close - PTS Stop;
```

Figure 15-10

The entry rules for the long trades require that the time is between the StartTime and FinishTime and that there have been less than one trade entry for the current day (set by the MaxDailyEntries input). The Open of the day must be greater than the Close plus the GapSize. GapSize is an input with a default value of 1. Next the strategy goes through Conditions 1-5. Conditions 1-5 were set in the Long Trend setups sections lines 52-65. Once all of the conditions are met then there is a limit order placed to go long at the next bar at the Close of yesterday minus the PenetrationPts. PenetrationPts is an input with a default value of 2 based on the Emini S&P.

The entry rules for the short trades require that the time is between the StartTime and FinishTime and that there have been less than one trade entry for the current day. The Open of the day must be less than the Close minus the GapSize. As stated in the previous paragraph. GapSize is an input with a default value of 2. It is the same for the long and short trades. The code could be changed so that there are two different inputs for GapSize so that one input would define the GapSize for the long trade and the other would define the GapSize for the short trades. Next the strategy goes through Conditions 6-10. Conditions 6-10 were set in the Short Trend setups section lines 67-81. Once all the conditions are met then there is a limit order placed to go short at the next bar at the Close of yesterday plus the PenetrationPts. PenetrationPts is an input with a default value of 2.

PenetrationPts is the same input for both the long and short sides. The code could be changed to set PenetrationPts so that there are two different inputs for PenetrationPts so that one input would define the PenetrationPts for the long trades and the other would define the PenetrationPts for the short trades.

The time based inputs for all trading systems are based on EST and should be changed to the time zone of the trading computer.

The last section that we take a look for this strategy is the Exit Code.

EasyLanguage Code in Tradestation, the flagship product of Tradestation Technologies

```
108
109   SetExitonClose;
110   SetStopContract;
111   If StpLs=True Then SetStopLoss(StpLsAmt);
112   If PrfTg=True Then SetProfitTarget(PrfTgAmt);
113   If DollarTrail=True Then SetDollarTrailing(DollarTrailAmt);
114   If Breakeven=True Then SetBreakEven(BreakEvenAmt);
115
116   If BarsSinceEntryExitLongs=True and BarsSinceEntry(0)>BarsToExitLongs
117       Then Sell This Bar on Close;
118   If BarsSinceEntryExitShorts=True and BarsSinceEntry(0)>BarsToExitShorts
119       Then Buy to Cover This Bar on Close;
120
121   If Time=LongExTime Then Sell Next Bar at market;
122   If Time=ShortExTime Then Buy to Cover Next Bar at market;
```

Figure 15-11

Any of the exit strategies can be set to False and "deactivated". The default exit strategy for this trading system is to only use a Stop Loss, Profit Target and Exit Time. The default inputs for the new updated code that would be used to match our original strategy would be:

244

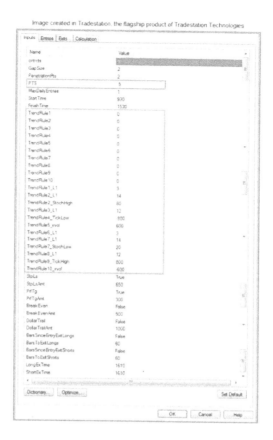

Figure 15-12

The new inputs are highlighted with a green box around them. The results of the strategy will still be the same with this set of inputs. The following inputs are "not in effect" unless the corresponding TrendRule is set to 1. For example if TrendRule1 is set to 1 then changing TrendRule1_L1 will affect the results of the strategy. If TrendRule1 is set to 0 then changing

245

TrendRule1_L1 will not affect the results of the strategy. This is true for TrendRule1 - TrendRule10. TrendRule1 - TrendRule5 are rules based on the long side while TrendRule6 - TrendRule10 are rules based on the short side.

We will first take a look at how each Trend Rule affects the strategy. There can be more than one TrendRule active at one time. All Trend Rules could be set to 1 and True in the strategy. The more rules that we set to 1 (or True), the fewer trades the strategy generates since each rule acts a "filter" or additional requirement for a trade setup.

The first rule, TrendRule1 is the long side of our Trend Rule 1 and is used to determine if the Close is greater than the daily close of L1 days ago. It is matched with TrendRule6 for the short side which is used to determine if the Close is less than the daily close of L1 days ago. For every TrendRule1 - 5 that is used to determine long entry trends, there is a matching TrendRule6 - 10 that is used to determine short entry trends.

When testing each set of Trend Rules the long and short combination for each pair are set to True by setting the inputs related to those pairs to 1 while the other inputs are set to 0. The combination of TrendRules based on the way the code is programmed is as follows:

TrendRule1 and TrendRule6

246

TrendRule2 and TrendRule7

TrendRule3 and TrendRule8

TrendRule4 and TrendRule9

TrendRule5 and TrendRule10

The individual Tradestation Performance Summaries for each rule combination with the results are shown next for the E-mini S&P in Chapter 4. Each performance report includes the original rules as well as each TrendRule combination (for longs and shorts) discussed in this chapter. The next five images show the results of how each TrendRule combination affects the results of the strategy. Notice the details such as the Average Trade Profit, Net Profit as a % of Drawdown, Profit Factor, and equity curve. These are some of the factors that I quickly notice and look at first when analyzing the quality of a trading system.

Chart created by Tradestation, the flagship product of Tradestation Technologies

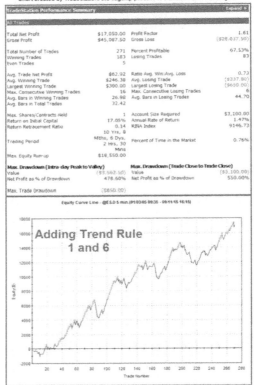

TradeStation Performance Summary			Expand ᵛ
All Trades			
Total Net Profit	$17,050.00	Profit Factor	1.61
Gross Profit	$45,087.50	Gross Loss	($28,037.50)
Total Number of Trades	271	Percent Profitable	67.53%
Winning Trades	183	Losing Trades	83
Even Trades	5		
Avg. Trade Net Profit	$62.92	Ratio Avg. Win:Avg. Loss	0.73
Avg. Winning Trade	$246.38	Avg. Losing Trade	($337.80)
Largest Winning Trade	$300.00	Largest Losing Trade	($650.00)
Max. Consecutive Winning Trades	16	Max. Consecutive Losing Trades	6
Avg. Bars in Winning Trades	26.98	Avg. Bars in Losing Trades	44.70
Avg. Bars in Total Trades	32.42		
Max. Shares/Contracts Held	1	Account Size Required	$3,100.00
Return on Initial Capital	17.05%	Annual Rate of Return	1.47%
Return Retracement Ratio	0.14	RINA Index	9146.73
Trading Period	10 Yrs, 8 Mths, 6 Dys, 2 Hrs, 30 Mins	Percent of Time in the Market	0.76%
Max. Equity Run-up	$18,550.00		
Max. Drawdown (Intra-day Peak to Valley)		**Max. Drawdown (Trade Close to Trade Close)**	
Value	($3,562.50)	Value	($3,100.00)
Net Profit as % of Drawdown	478.60%	Net Profit as % of Drawdown	550.00%
Max. Trade Drawdown	($650.00)		

Equity Curve Line - @ES.D 5 min.(01/03/05 09:35 - 09/11/15 16:15)

Adding Trend Rule 1 and 6

Figure 15-13

248

Chart created by Tradestation, the flagship product of Tradestation Technologies

TradeStation Performance Summary			Expand ⊌
All Trades			
Total Net Profit	$13,837.50	Profit Factor	2.41
Gross Profit	$23,662.50	Gross Loss	($9,825.00)
Total Number of Trades	136	Percent Profitable	72.06%
Winning Trades	98	Losing Trades	36
Even Trades	2		
Avg. Trade Net Profit	$101.75	Ratio Avg. Win:Avg. Loss	0.88
Avg. Winning Trade	$241.45	Avg. Losing Trade	($272.92)
Largest Winning Trade	$300.00	Largest Losing Trade	($650.00)
Max. Consecutive Winning Trades	17	Max. Consecutive Losing Trades	3
Avg. Bars in Winning Trades	30.12	Avg. Bars in Losing Trades	44.11
Avg. Bars in Total Trades	33.63		
Max. Shares/Contracts Held	1	Account Size Required	$1,012.50
Return on Initial Capital	13.84%	Annual Rate of Return	1.21%
Return Retracement Ratio	0.19	RINA Index	15599.65
Trading Period	10 Yrs, 8 Mths, 6 Dys, 2 Hrs, 30 Mins	Percent of Time in the Market	0.40%
Max. Equity Run-up	$14,850.00		

Max. Drawdown (Intra-day Peak to Valley)		**Max. Drawdown (Trade Close to Trade Close)**	
Value	($1,437.50)	Value	($1,012.50)
Net Profit as % of Drawdown	962.61%	Net Profit as % of Drawdown	1366.67%
Max. Trade Drawdown	($650.00)		

Figure 15-14

249

TradeStation Performance Summary			Expand ⌄
All Trades			
Total Net Profit	$8,812.50	Profit Factor	1.21
Gross Profit	$51,475.00	Gross Loss	($42,662.50)
Total Number of Trades	345	Percent Profitable	60.58%
Winning Trades	209	Losing Trades	129
Even Trades	7		
Avg. Trade Net Profit	$25.54	Ratio Avg. Win:Avg. Loss	0.74
Avg. Winning Trade	$246.29	Avg. Losing Trade	($330.72)
Largest Winning Trade	$300.00	Largest Losing Trade	($3050.00)
Max. Consecutive Winning Trades	9	Max. Consecutive Losing Trades	6
Avg. Bars in Winning Trades	21.84	Avg. Bars in Losing Trades	30.72
Avg. Bars in Total Trades	25.57		
Max. Shares/Contracts Held	1	Account Size Required	$4,087.50
Return on Initial Capital	8.81%	Annual Rate of Return	0.79%
Return Retracement Ratio	0.13	RINA Index	4800.33
Trading Period	10 Yrs, 8 Mths, 6 Dys, 2 Hrs, 30 Mins	Percent of Time in the Market	0.76%
Max. Equity Run-up	$10,512.50		

Max. Drawdown (Intra-day Peak to Valley)		Max. Drawdown (Trade Close to Trade Close)	
Value	($4,200.00)	Value	($4,087.50)
Net Profit as % of Drawdown	209.82%	Net Profit as % of Drawdown	215.60%
Max. Trade Drawdown	($650.00)		

Equity Curve Line - @ES.D 5 min (01/03/05 09:35 - 09/11/15 16:15)

Adding Trend Rule 3 and 8

Figure 15-15

250

Chart created by Tradestation, the flagship product of Tradestation Technologies

TradeStation Performance Summary   Expand

All Trades

Total Net Profit	$3,300.00	Profit Factor	1.60
Gross Profit	$8,925.00	Gross Loss	($5,525.00)
Total Number of Trades	47	Percent Profitable	72.34%
Winning Trades	34	Losing Trades	12
Even Trades	1		
Avg. Trade Net Profit	$70.21	Ratio Avg. Win:Avg. Loss	0.56
Avg. Winning Trade	$259.56	Avg. Losing Trade	($460.42)
Largest Winning Trade	$300.00	Largest Losing Trade	($650.00)
Max. Consecutive Winning Trades	8	Max. Consecutive Losing Trades	2
Avg. Bars in Winning Trades	24.85	Avg. Bars in Losing Trades	49.00
Avg. Bars in Total Trades	32.15		
Max. Shares/Contracts Held	1	Account Size Required	$2,412.50
Return on Initial Capital	3.30%	Annual Rate of Return	0.30%
Return Retracement Ratio	0.47	RINA Index	8645.70
Trading Period	10 Yrs, 8 Mths, 6 Dys, 2 Hrs, 30 Mins	Percent of Time in the Market	0.13%
Max. Equity Run-up	$3,425.00		

Max. Drawdown (Intra-day Peak to Valley)

Value	($2,650.00)		
Net Profit as % of Drawdown	124.53%		
Max. Trade Drawdown	($650.00)		

Max. Drawdown (Trade Close to Trade Close)

Value	($2,412.50)
Net Profit as % of Drawdown	136.79%

Equity Curve Line - @ES.D 5 min.(01/03/05 09:35 - 09/11/15 16:15)

Adding Trend Rule 4 and 9

Figure 15-16

251

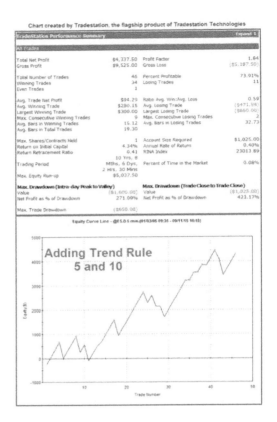

TradeStation Performance Summary			Expand ≈
All Trades			
Total Net Profit	$4,337.50	Profit Factor	1.84
Gross Profit	$9,525.00	Gross Loss	($5,187.50)
Total Number of Trades	46	Percent Profitable	73.91%
Winning Trades	34	Losing Trades	11
Even Trades	1		
Avg. Trade Net Profit	$94.29	Ratio Avg. Win:Avg. Loss	0.59
Avg. Winning Trade	$280.15	Avg. Losing Trade	($471.59)
Largest Winning Trade	$300.00	Largest Losing Trade	($850.00)
Max. Consecutive Winning Trades	9	Max. Consecutive Losing Trades	2
Avg. Bars in Winning Trades	15.12	Avg. Bars in Losing Trades	32.73
Avg. Bars in Total Trades	19.30		
Max. Shares/Contracts Held	1	Account Size Required	$1,025.00
Return on Initial Capital	4.34%	Annual Rate of Return	0.40%
Return Retracement Ratio	0.41	RINA Index	23013.89
	10 Yrs, 8		
Trading Period	Mths, 6 Dys,	Percent of Time in the Market	0.08%
	2 Hrs, 30 Mins		
Max. Equity Run-up	$5,037.50		
Max. Drawdown (Intra-day Peak to Valley)		**Max. Drawdown (Trade Close to Trade Close)**	
Value	($1,600.00)	Value	($1,025.00)
Net Profit as % of Drawdown	271.09%	Net Profit as % of Drawdown	423.17%
Max. Trade Drawdown	($850.00)		

Equity Curve Line - @ES.D 5 min.(01/03/05 09:36 - 09/11/15 16:15)

Figure 15-17

After reviewing all of the Trend Rules, Trend Rules 1, 2, 5, 6, 7, and 10 show the best improvement in the strategy. Trend Rules 4 and 9, which use the NYSE TICK rules, show good performance but not many trades are generated. In order to increase the number of trades for Rules 4 and 9, based on experience and not optimization, we changes the TrendRule4_TickLow to -800 (from 500) and TrendRule9_TickHigh to 800 (from 500). This

252

increases the number of trades since we allow long trades when the Tick has been lower on the day and allow short trades when the Tick has been higher on the day. Running the optimization for Return on Account, our results show that TrendRule4_TickLow has a best input as -1200 while TrendRule9_TickHigh has a best input as +900. The results for +800 and -800 are shown below. We like the consistency of these results.

Figure 15-18

Once we adjust the TickLow and TickHigh inputs, we can include Rule 4 and Rule 9 into our top list of rues. Keep in mind, the parameters for each of the Rules 1, 2, 5, 6, 7 and 10 are the default parameters. Each of these could be adjusted for further improvement in the strategy. Additionally, more rules could be added as there are many trend rules that could be used. These are just an example.

The rules are combined with the AND condition so if you start applying more and more rules set to True (1) at the same time, the more conditions you are requiring to be True at the same time and less trades will be generated. The rules could be combined with OR to make the strategy a strategy that will take trades if any of the rules are set to True (1).

If the goal is to generate many trades and the most Net Profit per contract in one system, then setting all of the Trend Rule inputs to 0 and not using a filter based on trend is the best approach. We like to be selective in our trading systems and like strategies with lower drawdown and higher average trade net profit. To increase trading frequency we add additional trading systems to our portfolio of strategies.

As previously mentioned, the optimization tool could also be used on the main TrendRule inputs by running an optimization from 0 to 1 for each of the TrendRule1-TrendRule10 inputs to see which combination of rules work best. Further optimizing the values of the "sub inputs" such as TrendRule1_L1, TrendRule2_L1, etc could also be done for an exhaustive test of the strategy. Be careful when optimizing since there are many perils of curve fitting a strategy so that it works perfectly in the past but performs poorly in the future. We rarely use the optimization tool and mainly use it to test the stability of a set of parameters by seeing how well the parameters next to our chosen parameters work. Our development is usually based on parameters that make sense from our observations of the market and the patterns that are developed in the market for which we are developing a trading system.

Setting it up in NinjaTrader

We setup the strategy in NinjaTrader using the following data and input settings. With all of the Trend Rule inputs set to False, the results should be the same as those in Chapter 4. Since there are additional data sets for this version that require more bars of daily data to load, there may be fewer trades at the beginning of the historical performance. Next are a series of screen shots that includes the data and input settings as well as performance summaries for Trend Rule 2 and Trend Rule 7 set to True. This is the best performing rule set with the highest average trade profit and nice equity curve. The code and setup video can be downloaded from our website. Chapter 16 has the details on the login information for our website to download the code and for viewing the instructional videos.

Figure 15-19

256

NinjaTrader 7 Gap Fill and Reverse MultiExit Input Settings

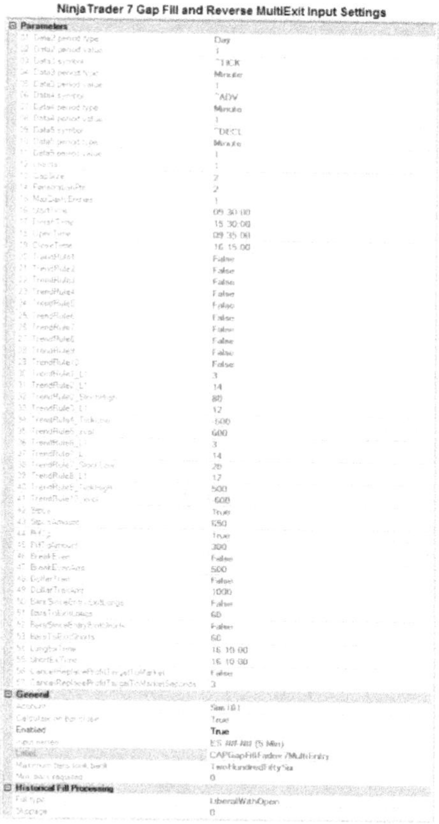

Figure 15-20

257

Gap Fill and Reverse in NinjaTrader 7 Performance Summary using the Stochastic Filter Rules 2 and 7

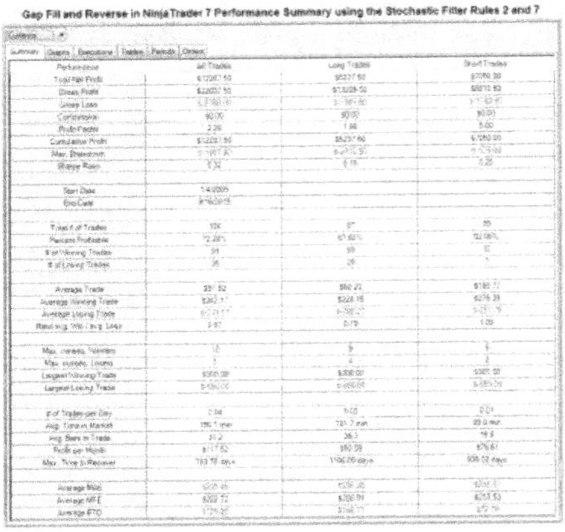

Figure 15-21

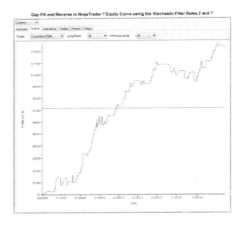

Gap Fill and Reverse in NinjaTrader 7 Equity Curve using the Stochastic Filter Rules 2 and 7

Figure 15-22

16.   Website and Code

One of the benefits offered in this book is a companion website with the open code available for download for both Tradestation and NinjaTrader. The companion website includes setup videos.
This website is at the following link:

 http://algorithmictradingsystemscode.com

There you will find the homepage. There is a page for each platform: Tradestation and NinjaTrader, where the code can be downloaded and instructional videos can be viewed. Each of these pages can be accessed with the password: algokingx777coder

The purchase of this book gives the individual reader the right to the site. The password is not for re-distribution or for sale.

With the publication of this book, my goal was to make more open code available for download than any other companion website I have seen. This site includes both the Tradestation Easylanguage and NinjaTrader's NinjaScript in C#. I encourage you to study the code to fully understand the strategy. If you are like me, you are more of a trader and market analyst than a coder but the one benefit of studying the code is that it will help you remove the biases in your trading based on the explicit nature of the description within the code.

If you do not have Tradestation, you can visit Tradestation at:

http://www.tradestation.com/

To gain access to the platform, you can open a trading account and fund it or you can setup a subscription account to pay for the use of Tradestation without having to setup a brokerage account.

If you do not have NinjaTrader, you can visit NinjaTrader at:

http://ninjatrader.com/

You can download the free version of NinjaTrader at the link above. You will need a data source and you will not be able to execute live trades without the purchase of a license but it is one way to get started at no cost.

17.   Conclusion

My original book, "Seven Trading Systems for the S&P Futures" published in 2010 shows how to setup Gap Fill and Gap

Continuation strategies for the S&P futures. These are strategies that I still trade with the most notable two being Gap Fill I and Gap Continuation II.

In this book, we have further developed automated trading algorithms based on gap strategies and expanded the number of futures markets for these strategies to markets such as the Bund, DAX, Euro Currency, and Crude Oil, as well as the E-mini S&P. The Gap Fill and Reverse trading system is a new counter trend strategy that we introduced in this book and add to our portfolio of trading algorithms to provide a diversity of trading system methodologies.

This strategy is based on a basic pattern and not on an indicator that uses optimized inputs. Over the years, many of my strategies have been pattern based (or a pattern with an indicator) as I find patterns have more stable walk forward results than systems based solely on indicators. Every system has draw downs and periods of time when it will not work as we see in the drawdown curve.

In Chapters 8 - 13, we paused and went over some of the Trading System Principles that we use the most in our strategy development discussing profit targets, stop losses, and how to apply popular trading rules such as "You can't go broke taking profits" and "Don't let a winning trade turn into a losing trade".

Towards the end of the book in Chapter 14, we went into detail on how to use and how to code multiple exits in a strategy and in Chapter 15, we discussed programming techniques and how to test strategies using multiple trend filters.

This book was written over a two year period with a great deal of attention to detail. It was an enjoyable challenge to provide this level of detailed trading system information in the form of a published book that includes programming code in more than one programming language. You can contact us from our book website at:

http://algorithmictradingsystems.com

or our main website at
http://capstonetradingsystems.com **About the Author**

Sophia Fosterhas been trading the financial markets since 1995 starting with stocks. He transitioned to futures and commodities in 1996 with an interest in the global macro view of the markets. In 1997 he began developing automated trading systems. He currently trades futures, equities, and options and has published several books since 2010. Algorithmic Trading Systems will be his fifth book. Trading, researching, and publishing are David's professional passions.

He is the owner of **Copy and Print,** a company that specializes in providing trading information and automated trading systems to its clients in the commodity, futures, forex, and stock markets. He has developed numerous trading systems since 1997 as well as the money management algorithms. The money management algorithms are the first commercially available "trading system for your trading system" that allows you to test different risk parameters and advanced entry techniques and setup automation in the same workspace setup. The mission is to provide trading systems that will exceed average returns while minimizing risk and meeting individual client's needs.

His formal academic studies include a BS in Electrical Engineering from Texas A&M University in 1994. He worked in government and corporate wireless telecommunications from 1995-2000 and became a full-time trader in 2001.

CPSIA information can be obtained
at www.ICGtesting.com
Printed in the USA
BVHW091312030621
608733BV00010B/2598